Janey

Janey

The Woman That Won't Shut Up

Janey Godley

**HODDER &
STOUGHTON**

First published in Great Britain in 2024 by Hodder & Stoughton Limited
An Hachette UK company

4

Copyright © Janey Godley 2024

A CIP catalogue record for this title is available from the British Library

Hardback ISBN 9781399728034
ebook ISBN 9781399728041

Typeset in Celeste by Hewer Text UK Ltd, Edinburgh
Printed and bound in Great Britain by Clays Ltd, Elcograf S.p.A.

Hodder & Stoughton policy is to use papers that are natural, renewable
and recyclable products and made from wood grown in sustainable
forests. The logging and manufacturing processes are expected to
conform to the environmental regulations of the country of origin.

Hodder & Stoughton Limited
Carmelite House
50 Victoria Embankment
London EC4Y 0DZ

www.hodder.co.uk

To my lassie, Ashley. Her love is everything.

PROLOGUE

The phone call that changed my life

'Janey, Doctor Wilson here,' said the voice on the end of the phone. 'We have the results of your bloods.'

My mouth went dry; I could hear my heartbeat in my ears. 'Are they ok?' I asked, dreading the response.

'Not really . . .' The doctor paused, briefly, before he delivered the news: '. . . there is a thing called a tumour marker and it's quite high—'

'Hang on, a tumour marker?' I repeated his words back to him, my voice trembling. 'What does that mean?'

'You need to go for a scan tomorrow, especially as we could feel something down in your abdomen.'

I blurted out the first thought that came into my head: 'I have a comedy tour on, can it wait?'

1

'No. I have called the Queen Elizabeth hospital for tomorrow. Nine a.m. Be there.' Cancer doctors, as I have since learned, do not beat around the bush.

I managed an 'ok, thanks' in response and hung up. I can't fully articulate how I was feeling right at that moment. I was numb for a few seconds, then the tears started.

I went through to the living room, where my husband, Sean, was watching telly. 'The blood tests came back with a high tumour marker,' I said through sobs. We both just stared at each other.

'Will you die?' Sean asked without blinking an eye. He has autism and doesn't cope well with shock or grief, so there is no filter or thoughtful words and big hugs as you see in the cancer movies from Hollywood.

My head was crammed full of questions and thoughts like, how far along is the cancer and where is this fucking tumour?! So Sean and I googled 'tumour marker' together – big mistake – and I had to scream into a pillow when I read what it indicated. Then I dried my eyes and put on makeup – I had a sold-out show in Perth that night. I couldn't let everyone down.

I called my agent and told him the news.

'I'm still doing the show tonight,' I said, terrified but determined.

'Are you sure?' Chris sounded worried. I had known him for years. He's more than just an agent, he's a pal.

I had two big sold-out shows left. My body was bloated and sore but I was convinced it would be ok, I could manage a few hours' work, it was afterwards when the show ended and I was left with what was inside my own head that I was worried about.

But when my tour manager Craig came to pick me up, I couldn't stop crying. I didn't care what anyone said. I hadn't even been diagnosed yet, but I knew it. I had cancer.

I felt as though I was dying that day; that night in Perth, I couldn't even tell you what I was saying onstage. The whole show was a blur, but I put on a brave face and did the first half. The only thing I remember vividly about that show was when I called my lawyer during the break and told him I had to get my affairs in order. A pretty morbid thing to do, I know, but I felt it was the only thing I could control at that moment.

The second half of the show went well, apparently. I got a standing ovation. I smiled, waved, thanked the audience, trying not to think about the excruciating pain in the bottom right side of my body, which felt like it was dragging me down towards the stage floor.

The next morning, shaking with fear, I headed to the Queen Elizabeth University Hospital, in the south-west of Glasgow, with Sean. I had the biggest show of the tour in Edinburgh at 7 p.m. that very night. I imagined

I would get a scan and it would be something small and fixable and I could get back on the tour bus and do the show. So, I prepared for the worst and hoped for the best.

Neither Sean nor I knew what to say to each other. For one of the first times in my life, I was quiet. I had been to the Queen Elizabeth before – it was the hospital my stepmum had died in – but I couldn't make sense of the place when I arrived. I was going through door after door, down corridors and round corners, until I finally arrived at the gynae clinic. But when I found the place, I couldn't bring myself to go in. I stood frozen outside the door and burst into tears – I knew this was going to be one of many hospital doors I would push open. I didn't want any of it to be real.

When I managed to stop crying, I was shown into a small, seated waiting room. I busied myself by blocking men who were trolling people who had tweeted about how much they enjoyed last night's show. The fluorescent overhead lights were giving me a headache and the smell of hand sanitiser nipped at my nostrils.

The staff reassured me they would do their best to look after me, and eventually I was shown into a side ward and told to undress my bottom half. Sean had to help me as I got my foot stuck in my leggings and I could hardly bend over to get my shoes off. He kept whispering

'It'll be ok Janey' like a mantra, but his face was pale and his hands were shaking.

So there I was, knickerless with my legs up in metal stirrups and a wand like a *Star Wars* lightsabre up my vagina as two solemn-faced doctors stared at a computer beside my head. I lay there petrified as they discussed the results on the screen.

I could see both doctors pointing and whispering to each other but all I could hear was my heart banging in my chest. Eventually, they looked up from the screen and faced me. They asked Sean and me to sit down on plastic seats together as they sat opposite us. It was like a nightmare speed-dating set up.

They explained, gently, that an 11-centimetre tumour was present on my right ovary. Sean and I looked at each other in panic.

I sat in that room stunned for a while. Then I wept buckets, again. The doctors sent me for a CT scan, and a porter pulled me backwards in a wheelchair down the hall, into the lift, through a multitude of corridors, and spoke to a female nurse about how he was going to leave and join the paramedics.

I had sent Sean home as this day was stretching out and he didn't need to be there for every second of it.

Meanwhile, over my head, the nurse and the porter had a full-blown conversation as I stared at my feet with my head down. Nobody spoke to me; from the moment that I had left the ward it was as if I suddenly didn't exist. He parked me in a busy room full of other people in wheelchairs and shouted 'Janey Godley' to the woman at the desk, then he left. Another man came and wheeled me in to the first – sadly not the last – scan of my life.

After I was taken back to the ward, a nurse came by and said, 'You have to call your husband back up as the doctor has seen the scan and wants to discuss it with you.'

That just floored me. I knew it was cancer, but each step that took me closer to hearing the official diagnosis was horrifying.

When Sean arrived, we sat on the hospital bed, looked out over the twinkling lights of Glasgow and held each other. We still couldn't think what to say. Because of Sean's autism, he often sings when he gets stressed out. So he burst into 'And so I face the final curtain!' I jumped off the bed, grabbed his mouth and shouted, 'No! Not that, not now. Stop that!' just as the doctor arrived to tell me about the scan. The doctor looked tired and stood for a pause, held both his hands out and said, 'Sit down, please.' This was like the worst improv scene I had ever witnessed. He was taking too long. The tension was too much, I just wanted him to blurt it out. Whatever it was just SAY IT NOW.

'No, just say it quick, please,' I replied, 'I don't want to hold hands or breathe slowly, I've just stopped him singing sad songs. I need you to tell me, is it cancer?'

'Yes, but let me explain,' he said as he sat down.

He said that they would need to wait until they operated to confirm, but all the signals showed it was most likely ovarian cancer.

Sean and I sat quietly. The doctor left and I sent Sean home again. I needed this time alone. I didn't want to have to deal with his grief and worry, I wanted to deal with my own.

I kept the room lights down low so I could see through the big window that framed all the lights of Glasgow twinkling down below. It made me think of how ironic life could be, as I was currently writing my first novel about a woman, Senga, who was dying of cancer, who would lie in her hospital bed and stare out at the Glasgow skyline. My next book must be about a woman who wins the lottery, I thought to myself and giggled.

I kept watching the lights twinkle all over Glasgow and I thought of Senga. Then I fell asleep.

1

PEOPLE ALWAYS ASK me why I went into comedy. I suppose they hear about my background and wonder how I ever found anything to laugh about. But they say tragedy plus time equals comedy, and I believe that.

My childhood was a tough one. I was sexually abused from a young age by my mum's brother, David Percy, who was in his late teens, and I coped by inventing an imaginary upside-down world. My big sister, Ann, was also being abused by him at the same time, but we didn't know what was happening to each other until much later in life. Experiencing sexual abuse at the hands of a family member was horrific and the effects of such trauma were long-lasting. I would self-harm, either by not eating properly or by ripping out bits of my hair and hiding them under the bed.

Living in Kenmore Street in Shettleston in Glasgow's East End with my two older brothers and one older sister was a bit of a crap time in itself. My dad Jim was hard-working, but my poor mammy Annie had a rough time of it with her mental health – she ended up in hospital as a result more than once.

Dad worked a decent job, but Annie seemed feckless with money. So, we kids were poor, often dirty, and walking about in shoes with holes in the soles. To this day we have no idea what our mum did with the cash our dad worked for. There were warrant sales when we were threatened with eviction; there were times Dad's wages were arrested in front of all his workmates at the factory. So, secrecy, poverty and abuse were rife.

But despite all the shit that was going on in our house, there was actually a lot of love and laughter, too. We were a family that laughed and joked and told stories – my brother David made me laugh louder than anyone and still does to this day. I know it's hard to imagine, but I was resilient and the most optimistic kid you could meet.

I never dreamed of becoming a comedian; I dreamed I would leave Kenmore Street and become an actress in the theatre. Just as my mammy, who loved musicals and film stars, pushed the furniture back on a Sunday afternoon to dance with Gene Kelly on the telly, I was dreaming of being onstage in plays or maybe in movies.

I never told anyone what I really wanted to be, but when I grew up and started working in the pub with my husband Sean in the eighties, I actually witnessed young guys in my bar get to work in film, thanks to Bill Forsyth and Paddy Higson creating workshops in the Dolphin Arts Centre in Bridgeton. That spurred me on – I reckoned if they could do it, so could I. How hard could acting be? I had been acting normal all my life.

But I never had the chance; I became a full-time publican, doing wee bits of extra work on TV, amateur drama and putting on plays in the bar. Then, in 1995, everything changed. My life got flipped on its head – it wouldn't be the last time either. Let me explain what happened.

After a particularly awful year of dealing with my husband's six brothers – think von Trapp family but without the happiness and the singing – Sean, our daughter Ashley and I walked away from the family business. It was a community pub, called the Weavers Inn, that made a healthy profit, and we owned the flats above, but it was in one of the roughest parts of Glasgow – The Calton. I had worked there since I was twenty; it was the place where Sean and I had essentially grown up, become business partners, and raised Ashley. But then my father-in-law died and, in the aftermath, Sean's six brothers took over the place.

While we were disputing their claim, they would become the owners and we would be their employees.

Bear in mind only one of the six actually worked in a pub, not to mention the fact that they already didn't like each other and certainly didn't like us. You can see the trouble coming, can't you?

It was a mess. There were nasty arguments, brothers taking sides, lawyers getting involved, all while builders and architects were waiting on instructions, as we had sunk a lot of our savings into renovating the place. It was a bonfire waiting to ignite, and I didn't know if my mental health – or my marriage – could take it.

The fear of failing and the fear of staying to make it work hit us like an emotional tsunami. Ultimately, for our own sanity we decided we had to leave. It meant we'd lose all the money we had already invested, but there was no other option. We took the financial hit and walked. I still get anxious when I think about it now. To this day, my husband still hasn't spoken to his family. It's been twenty-nine years.

It took the brothers months to get the bar opened and weeks for them all to start taking legal action against each other. Think the TV show *Succession* but without the nice suits and snappy dialogue. Meanwhile, my husband and I had to make the best of what we had left financially to try to make a stable life for Ashley, who was being ripped from her home and her family. It was a big decision, but I didn't want to be like the mother I'd had, one who was feckless and chaotic. I wanted Ashley to have stability and live without fear of her uncles.

Luckily, we had some savings left, so we bought a flat in Glasgow's West End. Despite the huge waves of anxiety, we were moving up in the world, for sure. It wasn't Kenmore Street and it was a long way from The Calton. Life in Glasgow's West End was so different from the east. The shops were very fancy, without bars or grilles on the window, and they opened later – there were shops near us that sold marble-topped kitchens and grocers who did organic couscous! – and the local area had great parks, museums, wonderful architecture, cosy pubs and nice places to eat.

The three of us arrived at our new home with nothing but a couple of black bags of clothes, toys and Ashley's schoolwork and uniform. We didn't have a chair, cup or spoon to our name – everything else had been left behind and we weren't going back to get it. We had to start from scratch, kitting out an empty house like we did when we were newly-weds.

Moving house was definitely exciting – if we tuned out the family drama. I got to pick out new furniture, paint schemes, all the things I never got to do in our old place. Plus, we had new, normal neighbours who weren't related to us, who didn't spit at me in the hallway or plot our downfall.

We were closer to Ashley's school as well, which meant she could get there by herself on the subway. She loved being independent and waving her off in the morning was great for me too, knowing I didn't have to rush back and open the pub. Sometimes I would wander up the road to the school to see her through the Victorian railings at lunchtime and have a chat with her.

I knew Ashley was having a tough time adjusting to her routine and life being completely out of whack. She was only eight years old; she didn't understand why everything was to be kept a secret, why we couldn't tell anyone where we were going or why we were running away. But we didn't want Sean's family to know where we were. Thankfully, my dad and stepmum Mamie were the bedrock of Ashley's life, always there to give her lots of extra love and attention. Mamie and Dad lived close and were such a positive, stable influence on our lives, lovely humans who doted on all their grandkids.

My dad started his life again getting sober in 1981 after leaving Mum and us in the mid-seventies. Dad and Mamie got married in 1984, two years after my mum Annie died. I believe my mum was thrown in the river in 1982 by her then on-again/off-again boyfriend Peter Greenshields. In 1978 he began a tumultuous, violent relationship with Mum that lasted four years, after he had got out of jail – he had been imprisoned for attacking other women. Poor Mum never stood a chance. I know it was Peter, but the police said there wasn't enough evidence to charge him. On the same day that she went missing, Peter stuck a knife in my brother David, who was arguing with him about Mum's disappearance. My brother got him charged for the attack and he ended up back in jail for a few years, though he managed to escape justice for my mother's death.

When Sean, Ashley and I moved to the West End, I didn't have a job; I thought, 'Fuck, what am I going to do?' I knew this was my one chance to try to make it, to try something I had always dreamed of doing. There was no way I could ask Sean to go out and get a new job. He couldn't work because a) he can't work for other people and b) his mental health was barely hanging on by a thread. So, it was my job to keep our family afloat.

I ran through my career options and, with no qualifications as I left school at sixteen years old, there wasn't much out there for me.

So, I decided to pick a career in which most people fail, despite having studied the craft for years.

I was going to try my hardest to make it as an actor, which on reflection is absolutely absurd. How naïve was I? I should have just got another pub job. Though living in the West End, that dream just felt closer, more accessible, because I could see it more in the world around me – I was up at the Ubiquitous Chip pub, mixing with all the actors and performers who stayed nearby (it was a bit of a creative hub back then).

I found out that, to be an actor, I needed an Equity card, and to get an Equity card I had to have stage time. So, I started doing open mic comedy just to bank some stage time. There was no way I could do music or magic, I was shit at both. But I come from a funny family, so it felt like comedy would be a good fit. Plus, I'd always been able to handle heckles and backchat from behind the bar.

2

IRONICALLY, I WASN'T really into watching comedy myself, not on telly or live gigs – I hadn't even been to a live comedy show before I started doing my own. I just wanted to do it because I thought I could. It didn't look that hard to me – telling jokes? That's easy, eh? And despite not having any experience or qualifications, I believed I could write my own material and become a performer. I mean, how hard could it be?

Very, as it turned out.

I started with a few open spots around the smaller pubs in Glasgow and the west of Scotland. There was barely ever an audience, the gigs didn't lead to much, and the pay was shite, but it was just brilliant to watch amazing comedians – alongside the crap ones – doing their craft.

One of my first gigs was at a place called the Halt Bar on Woodlands Road, near our flat. I saw they had a comedy night, so I just walked in and asked to speak to whoever was organising the gig. I was introduced to a bunch of young students and a guy called Billy Bonkers (yep, that was his name) and I secured a five-minute slot. I did okay, I didn't 'die on my hole', as they call it, so I thought, what else can I do to make this work?

There was a Polo Mint comedy competition at the time at the Third Eye Centre, which was a contemporary art venue in Glasgow. I entered and turned up in an outlandish outfit and over-the-top makeup – think Lily Savage without the wig.

It was a character act. I had a dog leash round a pillow with a face drawn on it and the whole act was about a woman who screamed a lot at her fake dog and mentioned all the tranquillisers her doctor had given her. Don't ask me what I was thinking, but I committed to it. So, I strutted into the arts centre and who was there but my wee daddy, sitting with his friends having tea.

'What are you doing, Janey?' he asked, clearly confused by the sight of his daughter with a face smeared in too much makeup dragging a pillow dog behind her.

'Comedy,' I replied.

He came into the auditorium and watched me scream at Pillow Dog and cheered when I won third place, despite the fact that only three people had entered the competition.

Dad never let me forget that event for years to come. How we laughed.

With each new gig and performance, no matter how small or seemingly inconsequential, I was putting myself out there, meeting new people – some brilliant comedians – and, when I stood backstage, I didn't feel like I was Janey who had no job, no pub and a very sleepy, sad husband at home.

I wasn't Mrs Janey Storrie anymore – I was Miss Janey Godley. I changed my name, and it made me feel like I had reinvited myself. Despite all the fear of moving house and trying to make money, I did feel strangely liberated. Nobody I was meeting knew who my husband was, nobody drank in my pub, and nobody was an ex-customer. I'd left the East End and I rarely met my old customers again.

I was making roads to meet other comedy promoters and try to hone my craft. There were brilliant comics I met from the very first day, including big Raymond Mearns, who I'm still friends with now. Raymond and I started out at the same time; both of us were EastEnders, both of us were doing gigs in the West End, both of us had a very similar sense of humour. I love Raymond.

I started doing comedy festivals in Glasgow, shows with Billy Bonkers, and regular gigs in Blackfriars, a comedy club in town. Claire McCauley ran that one;

she's an awesome woman who has always really supported comedians. She liked my stuff, even my early material, which was about the blue ink on sanitary towels in the TV adverts and how any woman who saw that would think she needed to attend the hospital, or that someone had drawn on her fanny pad. I also had material about being an angry mum and how the other mums at my daughter's posh school had never had sex up against a fridge. It wasn't the best material, but it got giggles.

Soon I started travelling around the country, and I even landed a few gigs in London. I couldn't believe it. But as exciting as it was to be out there, making it on my own, it was absolutely petrifying, too. It wasn't stage fright; I wasn't scared to perform in front of a room full of people – I'm not exactly shy. I was terrified because I went from having a full-time wage, having a business, having a cash flow, to living on my quickly shrinking savings and working for nothing as a stand-up.

You don't know how terrifying it is when you're travelling miles from home, forking out for a train ticket, staying with your pal because you can't afford a hotel, performing for pennies, in the hope that one day you'll get sixty quid for a gig, or you'll make it – which is ridiculous. I should have tried to get a normal job like a normal person. But I didn't know what else I could do, other than go and work in a pub, and I didn't want to stand behind another bar for the rest of my life.

At the same time, the best part *was* all the moving around, like some sort of nomad, staying in a flat in Edinburgh, or with friends in London or Dundee. I was couchsurfing as a fully grown adult who was married with a daughter at school. And I was getting better at being a comedian in the process.

Watching comics onstage in London was illuminating. I fully expected them to be a million times better than all the Scottish comics – some were, don't get me wrong – but I think being a comedian on a smaller circuit makes you work harder. I was stunned at some of the worst shite I had ever witnessed coming out of a human above a pub in Camden.

The good thing was, when I went to London, I was getting to discover it on my terms. I wasn't with a husband and a child, organising bus trips and tours of the city, looking after everyone else. I'd be living with my pal, Finlay, getting to walk the streets and understand the tube system on my own. I was meeting new people and getting to do what *I* wanted.

Being away from home was liberating. I was married at eighteen and running a pub a year later. I had been working fifteen-hour shifts for fifteen years, pretty much, with very little time off. Add school runs and raising a child to that, too. I had always been just a daughter, or a wife, or a mammy. Now, Ashley was being looked after at home, and I was on my own. It was like being the student I never got to be. And without Sean being awkward around people, I was making new friends.

So, I was somehow having the time of my life and feeling completely petrified all at once. And as happy as I was to be doing something that I loved, I felt awful guilt about leaving Ashley. I should've been at home, I should've been focused on earning a better wage, and I should've been a better mammy, but I was too busy enjoying freedom, because I had never experienced it to this extent before.

Ashley was only eight years old – she still didn't understand why we had taken her away from everything she knew, and she had loved some of her uncles, as awful as her dad and I knew them to be. It was a lot for a child to deal with, let alone understand, and the big changes and all the secrecy made her incredibly anxious. She became a real telly addict and would often repeat adverts word for word while doing her homework. Sean would do this repetitive linguistic thing too – I think I thought it was funny, but in hindsight I can see that Ashley was displaying autistic tendencies herself, and I had no idea.

I knew that her dad was doing his best, but I was aware that he was emotionally adrift too. Sean had such a difficult time adjusting to our new life. He sank into his own terrible, great depression. His father was gone two years now, but there had been no grieving – the Storrie family don't do grief; they do wills, money, lawyers and treachery. On top of that, my husband had lost his job, his pub, his flat and a lot of his money. He was lost, himself. In fact, I couldn't see it at the time, but my husband was slowly having one of the biggest breakdowns of his life. And that was something I completely missed. I didn't fully appreciate the effect his family turning on him and his abandoning them would have on his mental health. I had no idea he was descending into another suicide attempt. I was too busy trying to earn a few quid at a gig to look at what was actually happening in my own family. I suppose I missed so much that was staring me in the face.

It was hard for Sean and me to adjust to what my new work dynamic meant for my marriage as well, because at the pub my husband was also my boss, and I was his worker. Now, I was my own boss, I wasn't working under his supervision as I had been for most of my adult life, he wasn't there to see what I was doing, or micromanage me the way he always had. Bearing in mind we didn't know he was autistic then – we just thought he was irritating.

But we got to go to Disneyland that year, the three of us as a family. The first holiday ever where we didn't have that pub in the back of our mind, because every single time we went on holiday there was either a fire in the pub, or one of the brothers barred the best customers, or there was a fight, or somebody screwed the money, or somebody kicked the jukebox. Now we didn't have to phone every day with a special phone card – cos it was the olden days – to try to find out what was happening. It was our first stress-free holiday.

And there was another exciting milestone that summer – my first foray into the Edinburgh Fringe.

3

I REMEMBER IT well. I knew the Fringe was where so many of the great comics had started, so my new pal, Johnny Vegas, whom I'd met through the Glasgow comedy open spot circuit, and I decided to enter the Gilded Balloon's *So You Think You're Funny* competition. A bunch of us piled into the wee blue pub van Sean still had and headed along the M8 to Edinburgh. It was my first proper experience of the festival, other than a day when Sean and I walked through the Royal Mile, thirteen years before in 1982.

I was super excited, but also so nervous that I spilled a pint of water all over the floor and down Johnny's giant, brown crimplene flares that he wore as part of his costume. Thankfully it didn't affect his performance – Johnny was noticed that day, and I was so pleased for him. My gig went ok, I got some big laughs and some nice comments from the judges, but I wasn't placed in the heat.

Nevertheless, I was still determined to make it in comedy, so I decided to go back to the Fringe the following year, and this time I stayed with some new pals who were working on the famous stage show *The Phantom of the Opera*, which was in town. I was staying in a flat down near Leith Walk, and Ashley and her dad came and stayed with me for a few days while I tried out some open mic gigs.

There was a big tent for Fringe Sunday and I was booked to do a slot. I was so excited. Ashley was sat in the front row with her hair in bunches and wearing her favourite dungarees, looking like butter wouldn't melt. The act before me was a lady in a shimmering green dress with a fish bowl on her head, singing weird songs. Standing backstage, I could hear the other acts talking about a determined heckler in the crowd. I peeped round the curtain and there was Ashley standing up shouting, 'Your fish is dead' as she pointed at the bowl on the woman's head. She was right – the plastic fish was on its side sloshing about in the water.

'Oh no, that's my kid,' I said to the MC. I wasn't surprised that she was a good heckler, I was impressed at her confidence, but she always was a funny kid; even back in the pub she knew how to get a laugh. And it was good to see her shout back at adults – it was a long time coming after all she had been through. The MC laughed and brought me onstage, which was when Ashley stood up again and shouted, 'That's my mum and she promised to take me on holiday but I have been sat here looking at dead fish and eating chips. Come on Janey tell us a joke!' The audience howled with laughter and I dragged her out of the tent. It was funny; people thought it was a double act or a very creepy ventriloquist show.

Then that night, Ashley became really unwell. So, in the middle of the festival, I had to take her to the Edinburgh Children's Hospital. I was so glad I was there, but it made me realise that maybe I wasn't the mammy that I should have been. Looking back, I can see that I wasn't paying enough attention to my daughter, and that will always be something I regret and carry with me. She needed me and her dad to be focused on her and we weren't. Ashley was ok, in the end, but I still felt this awful, all-consuming guilt. As her parents, we were all over the place – me physically, and Sean emotionally.

For a while, my husband had been having episodes of just sleeping all day. All I can remember about him back then was that he slept a lot. I remember he slept really heavily one week when I was in Edinburgh, and he called me on one of those days to say that Ashley hadn't come back from her trip up to the shops on Byres Road.

I got the next bus back to Glasgow, completely frantic, and it was like that Keanu Reeves film *Speed*, I didn't let the driver stop at any of the bus stops on the way. It turned out that while her dad was sleeping Ashley had gone up the West End, two subway stops away, to spend her pocket money, but when it came to one o'clock she didn't phone him with her special phone card as she usually did. Ashley wasn't the kind of kid who just wandered off or didn't come home. She was extremely diligent and, to be honest, too well behaved. So obviously I thought the worst. I imagined she'd been abducted, or that his family had taken her, or somebody had killed her – after all my mammy was murdered, so I knew these things could happen.

I was petrified, Sean was beside himself, and my dad, God love him, was running around the West End showing people her photo, trying to find her in the subway stations.

Staring out of my bedroom window frozen with fear, I fell to my knees and prayed to a God I didn't believe in. 'Please let her be ok,' I begged out loud, over and over again. Where the hell was she?

I called the police and reported her missing. Having to answer so many questions while your heart is beating in your ears and your blood is rushing like ice water through your veins is next to impossible. The police assured us that she was probably just out playing with pals and would turn up eventually. They weren't that worried; I suppose the West End of Glasgow police were slightly less nervy than the East End's cops.

After what felt like days, my dad found her on the street. She walked right into him. He was hysterical and scared her with his frantic hugs. It was only then that Ashley realised how long she had been away.

She'd gone into a garden in the street behind her school, met a family who were having a picnic, and learned to ride a bike. Then she decided, I've had enough of that, I'll wander down the hill and get the subway home. By that time, it was five o'clock and she'd been missing for four hours.

I think, in a way, it was good that my dad found her because he had been dealing with a tremendous amount of guilt and trauma as a result of the child abuse I had suffered at the hands of my uncle. He had never really forgiven himself for not being there for me. At least he got to save one child, even if it wasn't his own.

Back at the Fringe, I got a ten-minute slot at the famously rowdy Late 'n' Live gig and I was determined to show off my shouty comedy skills.

I remember it so well. The show opened and the crowd roared as the MC introduced the first act. I stood at the back of the room, watching these two naked men walk onstage carrying a plank of wood. Nothing was happening, just two men walking about with their balls hanging out. The audience was bemused and booing. They were getting angry, but the two naked men didn't seem to care and carried on walking about with their plank of wood.

The comedy promoters next to me were screaming with laughter, clapping and shouting, 'Genius!' and I realised, in that moment, that I would never understand comedy and it probably wasn't something I should try to do. Too late – I was on next.

I walked out into the smoke-filled room, the raucous crowd hushed, my heart was in my mouth, and someone shouted: 'Aw fuck, it's a woman!' I stared them down and said, 'I would have got my cock out, but the men would be jealous,' as I pointed to the naked arses leaving the stage. The crowd burst out laughing. I finally breathed out, enjoyed my ten minutes at Late 'n' Live, and lived to tell the tale. I was a brand-new comic, but you know what? I had jokes.

When my time was up, I ran through the crowd to see the promoter, fully expecting to be told that I was good. If only. The promoter scowled at me as I approached. 'You were too rude,' they said, 'nobody wants to hear jokes about women's vaginas.' Still glowering, they walked away to the bar with some famous comics I had seen on the telly. I was so embarrassed.

I caught the last bus back to Glasgow. Clearly, I had a lot to learn. And learning all the ins and outs of the Edinburgh Fringe was a huge feat in itself. Pre-internet days, you had to send a huge video cassette with a cover letter to a venue in the hope they would agree to take most of your money off you. That's basically what happened – the business model was like no other. You paid them in advance for the seats, then when an audience came in they gave you back SOME of the cash you'd paid. There were extra costs too – you had to pay hundreds of pounds to get into the Fringe brochure, hundreds for the venue's PR (even though they didn't necessarily do PR for you), you had to pay for a tech to work the mic and on top of all that there was the added expense of posters, flyers, adverts, and the flat in Edinburgh usually cost a few thousand pounds for the three and a half weeks (even in the nineties – it's worse today). You'd be lucky to recoup any of that, and bear in mind up until about 2005 Scottish acts rarely got reviewed or mentioned in the press. So, we comedians who lived in Scotland struggled to get an audience or even some decent coverage. Yet we kept doing it! Thankfully we now have the internet to advertise shows and the Free Fringe venues where you don't have to sell your kidney just to perform.

As well as performing at the Fringe that year, I continued going back and forth to London to try my hand at some open mic gigs. Scotland's clubs were getting better, but the one that had real clout, The Stand, barred me for asking why they had a nefarious rule that if you worked there one week you couldn't work at any other comedy club for two weeks either side, which was insane! How were you supposed to make money and build a name for yourself if a club inhibits you? So, I went to the actors' union Equity (yes, I did get my Equity card, but still no acting work), and they complained on my behalf to the club, but it didn't change anything, it just meant that I was barred from the only decent club in Scotland. I didn't know this rule was used in many chain comedy clubs around the world. Why was I so fucking argumentative? Why couldn't I just shut up and go with the flow? Maybe I was missing the combative atmosphere of the pub and Sean's family.

I thought that if I went to London, maybe I would get a big agent or the TV people might see me and I'd get my big break. That optimistic spirit I had as a kid never left me. I stayed with my old pal, Finlay, who ran restaurants in Butler's Wharf, the fancy area behind Tower Bridge.

I did an open spot at the famous Comedy Store in central London. Back in the nineties, the Comedy Store didn't have many women on the bill – it was always harder for women to get a slot there than men – so I felt an enormous amount of pressure. My nerves were absolutely jangling, standing backstage in the most famous comedy club in the UK. I must have peed about sixteen times in the tiny toilet, but the lovely Bill Bailey, who had seen me MC in Paisley the year before, treated me with such kindness and reassured me I'd be fine. I didn't believe him; I was sure I would mumble shite and die a death out there.

Mark Lamarr, the guy off *Never Mind the Buzzcocks*, was hosting, so I was utterly starstruck, and on top of that my knees were wobbling and my heart was thumping all the blood through my body with enough force that I could feel it. After an eternity, my name was introduced, and I walked out onstage and did my five minutes. It's really hard to perform for such a short amount of time, condensing all your good material into tiny bite-size pieces. My act just wasn't a 'one liner' type of show.

Some of the audience booed when I said was Scottish and one guy shouted, 'Fuck off home!', which made me giggle – I hadn't faced that before. But I carried on and managed to get my short slot out of my mouth without having a heart attack. It wasn't great – I was interrupted a few times, and having only five minutes to recover and then squeeze in the rest of the material was a hard juggling act. After the show, the guy who appraises the acts came backstage and told me I shouldn't have done the abortion material as I lost the audience.

'I don't have abortion material . . .' I replied, confused. But he told me to stop arguing and listen to him. I stared at him in silence. To this day, I have no idea what he was talking about; I think I have covered everything else from abuse to murder in comedy, but not abortion. I genuinely think he got me mixed up with the guy who was on after me who had a joke about his girlfriend getting an abortion.

I never got asked back to that club, which was a shame because I wrote six abortion jokes just in case. That hot summer night in London, I walked through the hazy city, slowly meandering back to Finlay's flat, dreading telling him that I failed to make a hit at the Comedy Store. Such is life in comedy.

Despite that knock-back, I loved London – the views, the food, the history of the city; walking the cobblestoned streets and sitting by the Thames watching the river flow by as I ate lunch on a terrace. The London comedy circuit was much more vibrant than the Scottish one, too, and meeting so many amazing comedians and people I had seen on the telly was equal parts wonderful and nerve-wracking. I remember one particularly impactful night that has stayed with me until this day.

I was about to go onstage and do my usual shtick: some funny stuff about being a mum, and that joke about blue ink being the colour of blood on sanitary pads in adverts (I really thought that was hilarious back then). But just before I went on, I met the comedian Stewart Lee, who was lovely, and we chatted for a while. I told him what had been happening in my life recently, the drama with the pub, and stories about my husband's sometimes hilarious but odd behaviour. He looked at me and said: 'Stop telling jokes and tell the audience what you just told me, tell them your truth.' So I did.

I stood onstage and told that room in London what it was like to be a working-class mum with a kid at a private school; what it was like to have the cops hunt your house for guns because you married into a dodgy family. I made it funny. They laughed. I told them I had a creepy uncle as a kid and made them laugh about that too. It was like something unlocked in me. Thanks for that, Stewart.

It was different doing comedy in the nineties. We obviously didn't have phones with maps. I had a basic mobile from BT that was like a pound bag of sugar in my pocket, but we still used payphones as they were cheaper. Everyone just turned up for gigs having emailed or called to arrange them a month earlier; we all carried a London A–Z book to find streets and tube stops to get to gigs. Buses were important on a budget and having good mates who put you up was a lifeline.

I still have a soft spot for London. Back then, I loved it for selfish reasons – mostly getting away from the stresses and strains of family life, which makes me feel awful now. I wish Sean had been better and Ashley would have had more stability, but I had to work, I had to find a way to make a living that made all of the struggling worthwhile.

And I was getting there. Slowly but surely, I was beginning to make a name for myself in comedy. I won the Paisley Comedy Award in June 1997, and then as a result of the award, I became a weekly host at Mr P's comedy venue. It was a proper Paisley pub and a real rough and ready crowd, but they showed me so much love and support every week, which will carry me for ever. I learned so much from those years hosting the gig and loved having guests like Phil Kay, Parrot and Fred MacAulay on their wee stage.

But as well as well as working towards my future, I had to confront my past. I had to confront my worst nightmare. My uncle.

4

DAVID PERCY, MY mother's brother, was finally caught by the cops on a warrant. In 1997 he was to face me and my sister in court on charges of historic sexual abuse. He was never far from my mind, and just the thought of seeing him was utterly terrifying. This man had sexually traumatised us back in the late sixties and early seventies and we had finally reported him to the cops in early 1992, after a journalist who wrote about the abuse we had suffered told me I could still charge him.

The day of the trial came around, and it was the moment I'd been dreading. My sister and I were numb with fear. We had many, many meetings with the procurator fiscal, but they didn't answer any of our pretrial questions. In fact, every time we spoke they kept changing plans about how to proceed in the trial, and they kept switching prosecutors, which meant my sister and I would have to keep regurgitating all our previous conversations over and over again. We knew my uncle had a good relationship with his lawyer, yet we couldn't form a decent relationship with the one person who was going to be tackling the worst event in our lives. It's hard enough going to trial with a historic abuse case without the case being handed back and forth between procurator fiscals who haven't invested enough time to understand our background.

The police had made it clear that my sister, Ann, and I were never to discuss the case with each other so we couldn't be accused of collaboration, which would put the trial in jeopardy. The result of this trial would change how we lived our lives for ever, and, to be honest, I was starting to lose faith in the justice system. But my sister and I followed all the rules and prepared to do something completely alien to us and hope for the best.

We all had to go to the new big court building just south of the River Clyde and sit and wait in a witness room on the ground floor. There was my sister Ann, my dad Jim, my brother David and my stepmum Mamie, each one of us nauseous with nerves. We saw David Percy enter the court building – he was caught by photographers as he walked in. His entourage, who were dressed in football tops, were shouting and swearing at the press. My family sat quietly watching through the glass doors as two women came up to the door and shouted threats at us. We could hear them through the glass quite clearly. I saw the court officials moving them on and heard the rustling static noise of their shell suits as they shuffled away down the corridor.

It was, all in all, pretty horrifying. My sister and I both felt we needed more help from the police, but they were just detectives focusing on the law and the charges, they weren't there for emotional support. They told us to try to stay unemotional, speak clearly and tell the truth. That was the best they could do.

My name was called and I hugged my dad and walked through the glass doors and along the corridor to face the big brown door that would lead me into the courtroom. The cop on the door was a local policeman I knew called Fred who used to come to The Calton on his rounds. Seeing a familiar face absolutely helped me in that moment. 'You can do this, Janey,' he said.

My knees wobbled as the big door slammed behind me. The roof of my mouth dried up and I thought my tongue wouldn't work. My heart was beating a tattoo in my chest as I stared at David Percy in the stand opposite me. I watched the jury watch me and every nerve in my body jangled.

The defence lawyer started with a few basic questions like 'Do you remember living in Kenmore Street as a child?' and then proceeded to make me sound like a child who wanted attention from my uncle and that's why I told bad stories about him. The anger bubbled inside me as though I was a volcano waiting to erupt, but I remained calm and explained that I didn't need extra attention from a man who likes to sexually hurt children. I wanted to climb out of the witness box and punch him. But I had to stay focused.

The entire jury was a blur, and I was petrified to make eye contact with them in case they thought I was too bold or too strong. It's hard to get that sort of situation right when all you have for reference is a plethora of American courtroom dramas. So, I spent my time in the witness box staring at the man who held me down to sexually assault me when I was five years old.

He wouldn't look me in the eyes, he just kept his head down. Every time his defence called me a liar, I suggested that, if he trusted my uncle so much, 'Why don't you leave your kids with him?' The judge glared at me and told me to answer the defence.

The lawyer repeated the question: 'Are you a liar?'

'You are paid to call me a liar,' I said, 'and even if you believed me, you would still call me a liar. That's your job.'

Reliving such a painful part of my past in front of strangers was horrendous. Saying the words, 'He put his fingers inside my vagina' to a man who basically spent hours calling me a liar was absolutely the worst. I had to explain in very precise detail the way my uncle touched me and the parts of my vagina that he hurt – you have to use the proper anatomical language or else charges can be dropped. But though I was shaking, I wasn't embarrassed. I was on a roll. I spoke very clearly about every single sexual act that dirty bastard had inflicted on me thirty years before. I didn't flinch. I could see the jury out of my peripheral vision looking at him as he kept his head down. This was one gig I wasn't going to mess up.

David Percy pleaded not guilty. He denied ever touching me or my sister. His defence was that, because I was a comedian, I was just an attention-seeker who wanted even more. I reminded his defence that I had medical records going back to the sixties that indicated abuse and urinary issues, so that was some long game I was playing. What defence he used for my sister I will never know. I never asked her and I wasn't in court when she gave her evidence.

The trial lasted a few days during the week, then spilled over a weekend. I was utterly emotionally exhausted but, every night when I went to bed to try to sleep, I was frozen with fear that my uncle would be found not guilty and my sister and I would have to face all those people who had defended him and called us liars.

Once my brother and dad had given evidence we never returned to the court. My sister and I sat tight in my flat on the Monday as we awaited the verdict. When we found out that the jury had reached their decision, 'guilty on all charges', I wept.

The relief was overwhelming. He was sentenced to two years as it was his first sexual offence, although I've read online since that he had been in trouble with the law before for guns and something to do with supporting loyalist paramilitaries in Northern Ireland in the late eighties. Now he was off to prison and on the sex offenders register. I didn't care about the light sentence – I was just pleased my sister and I were vindicated and we could move on with our lives. It was finally over.

Despite how stressful a time it was for us all, despite my having migraines and sleep terrors, to this day it is one of the best things I have ever done. I cannot thank my sister Ann, my brother David, and my husband Sean enough for the support and determination they showed in helping me through that horrible week. We got through it, together. My dad even celebrated being fifteen years sober after having a heart bypass soon after.

Two days after the verdict, I was on a high and back in London doing gigs. That was when I met someone incredible through Finlay, someone who was to become an amazing pal, who would be with me to this day.

She was tall, also Scottish, with red curly hair and the biggest personality I have ever encountered. Her name was Monica Brown, and we were instant pals – we just gelled on meeting. She lived in London, so she would come to gigs with me whenever I was in town. Those early days are something we still look back and laugh about – me onstage, her chatting up some bloke in the crowd, us grabbing a cab down to the Atlantic Bar and having the best night ever. Monica's ability to attract the strangest man in the room was legendary and my ability to tell him to fuck off was equally worthy of a mention. She could hold a conversation with a brick wall, whereas I've just never been all that sociable. Even though my job is pretty much talking to people for a living, offstage I've never been good at networking or the social side of things. I mostly turned up at clubs, pulled off my anorak, walked onstage and did my show, then left straight after my slot was finished. I didn't drink much, so I wasn't really the party girl either. If my success was down to making pals I would never work again.

Monica quickly became my staunchest ally. She gave me perspective on my marriage and my career and spoke to me about stuff I had never discussed before, like feminism and politics. You see, I had never had a girl pal before in my adult life. I never had someone who challenged my beliefs, or my attitude. I never had a woman tell me I looked great and that I deserved more.

She was a powerhouse pal, and I am so glad I met her. I realised I had missed a strong female presence in my life, and now I had found one I wasn't letting her go. Monica told me years later that she loved being with me but sometimes, back then, it felt like I had decided she was going to be my pal and nothing would stop that from happening. She says I kidnapped her! I am so glad I did.

One hot summer night in London, we were heading to a gig I was doing off Oxford Street. We were laughing and chatting incessantly as usual, until Monica stopped walking and started screaming and pointing at the ground in front of us. There was a tiny – and I mean a baby – mouse running along the side of the pavement. Monica screamed. As it was London obviously nobody batted an eye, and thank God because with all the screaming she then vomited and I laughed so hard I peed myself. We turned up to the venue, her curly hair stinking of vomit and my jeans piss-stained. I did the gig anyway.

Those years in the late nineties were full of London gigs – which were going well as folk seemed to like me there – and summers spent at the Fringe.

The Fringe was always hard work. I was out there flyering every single person I walked into, I spent hours upon hours handing out those wee flappy bits of paper all over Edinburgh and begging people to come see my show at eleven at night. The first flat I had rented was a tiny, expensive, Victorian tenement up about 800 stairs in the New Town. After over twenty-five years of doing the Fringe, two things have become apparent.

- It would have worked out cheaper to have bought a flat in Edinburgh back in 1996.
- Almost every flat I rented was up the top of 800 stairs.

Still, I wouldn't have changed a thing. To this day I still get tingles looking at the stunning ancient buildings in Edinburgh and I am happy to know that Ashley and I spent twenty-five summers there, watching her grow up and watching us become the best comedy team ever. The memories are precious, although I am sure she has her own tale to tell of putting up with both the exhausting work and an embarrassing mum.

Ashley started doing comedy when she was eleven years old. She launched the Improv Club in London (it shut down soon after) and she took a show to the Fringe in 1999 called *What Were You Doing When You Were 13?* It was amazing to watch her confidence onstage; the fact we were both doing the same job made me so happy.

Ashley could improvise as well as any pro and she had no problems speaking to adults as she had spent her early life chatting to punters in our pub.

Her show was a great idea. She had two guests a day onstage – usually other comedians at the Fringe – and she played music from the year they were thirteen years old. She asked them what toys they played with and what kind of things were on telly at that time and at the end the audience had to guess what the year was. Even at thirteen years old she was a great communicator and a funny interviewer. I had a show across town in a small venue where we were struggling to get an audience, and every day Ashley's show was sold out. It got loads of press and global attention, and she even landed guest spots with the likes of Peter Kay, who was doing a Fringe show that year. But despite the great reviews, after that Fringe Ashley swore she'd never do stand-up again. 'It's not my thing,' she said. Ashley was, and is to this day, a brilliant comedian. She's a natural.

5

MY SCHEDULE WAS getting busier and busier, and at the start of the millennium I was approached by a guy who owned a big cafe bar called Mansions at Charing Cross in Glasgow, to start my own comedy club. It was a step in the right direction. I wasn't going to get work at the local big comedy club – I was still barred after I had debated their booking policy, and the situation had turned nasty. I was told that someone at the club told other comedy promoters that I wasn't funny; apparently they even made spurious claims that I was a 'drunk' and difficult to work with – I'm not even a drinker.

It became a 'Them and Us' situation with some of their regular acts being forced to take sides. I understand my speaking out upset the clique who were loyal to the club.

Mansions was a brilliant venue, huge through the

back, and could seat over eighty people. So, we did a weekly gig and I was MC. Ashley was taking tickets and Sean did the seating and sound for me. It wasn't great-paid work, but I was making some cash and we were managing on a budget and our savings. MCing a gig is a great way to get stage time, think up material and get wonderful experience.

I didn't really want to be a comedy promoter to be honest; it felt like everything I'd left behind in running a pub again. And being a comedian who runs a gig in one city can be a pain as it means you can't really work elsewhere in the meantime. So I was conflicted. I was determined to be a national comic, not just a Glasgow one. Plus, the gigs still weren't in abundance at home. I never got any work there or on *The Live Floor Show,* the new comedy show on BBC Scotland. That's what you get for speaking out and being the person that everyone wants to shut up.

The good news was, I was headlining over most of the acts who spent time snarking at me. We sometimes performed together in other clubs and watching them flounder with new audiences outside of their wee comedy gang hut was the sweetest revenge – I never seemed to struggle in front of new audiences.

Although sometimes this came back to bite me. If one of the guys hadn't had a good gig, it would automatically be my fault. A part of me used to dread going on because if the audience really liked me the guys would feel like I had 'stolen laughter' off them, so I would get the silent treatment in the green room, or they would say things like, 'You can talk about your fanny and get the laughs, I suppose,' as if they never once mentioned their genitals. Of course, that's absurd, but I remember how, in those early years, some of those Scottish male comedians really made me feel anxious and isolated at times. As the years went by, I stopped making myself small and just got better and better – it was up to them to deal with their own insecurities.

Anyway, I had my own club at Mansions and was booking fabulous acts like Reginald D. Hunter, my old pal Raymond Mearns, Ross Noble and Craig Hill. Hosting and getting so much stage time was, and still is, the best way to gain comedy chops. Unfortunately, Mansions closed its doors when the owners lost the venue, so it was back to gigging up and down the country for me.

Before long, I was headlining smaller clubs throughout the UK and making plans to head to the New Zealand comedy festival. If I wasn't getting much work in Scotland, then I would go to the other end of the world and try my luck there.

I had heard good things about the New Zealand comedy scene from other comics as we chatted backstage at gigs. Entering the festival would be a baptism of fire to see if my comedy worked abroad.

So I sent them an email, fully expecting to be refused. Why would they accept a show from a complete unknown from Scotland who wasn't even being brought over by a promoter? But to my complete and utter surprise, I was accepted. I had to send so much paperwork – hard copies by airmail (something that's done by literally one email and a link now), and then applied to the New Zealand High Commission for a work permit.

I couldn't wait to get there. I had to finance my own flight and hotel but the festival applied for some grants from the British Council to help me. The Creative Scotland arts funding body refused to help; they didn't finance comedy, just opera, theatre and ballet. So I had to be good with my budget.

Leaving my family behind to make such a huge trip was incredibly daunting, and I was worried I was making a reckless decision. But Sean and I spoke at length about the costs and the opportunity versus income and outgoings. He really pushed for me to go, as did Ashley, who kept joking, 'If it's good don't come back, just send for me.' Even my dad stepped in to show his support – he insisted on paying for the flight, which was a really big deal. 'Make sure you make them laugh loud,' he said to me.

I landed in Singapore first and was stunned by the beautiful Changi Airport, with its amazing food courts and an actual butterfly garden. I still remember checking into the hotel that I had booked for the layover, and watching TV at 5 a.m. with jetlag. The programme was *Gilmore Girls*; I didn't even know if we got that in the UK then, but I was hooked. I lay in bed wanting to phone home, but resisted the urge as I didn't know what time it was and I hadn't bought a phone card. Luckily the hotel had a business centre, so I emailed home to let the family know I was safely halfway round the world.

The second leg of the flight all the way to Auckland was so long I felt like I was going to the moon. I gawped at the snowy caps of mountains from the aeroplane window, and I was squirming in my seat to try to get a good look at Auckland as the plane was coming in to land. I could barely sit still, I was so excited. The festival organisers sent one of their assistants, a lovely woman named Rosie, to pick me up (we're pals to this day!).

Auckland is absolutely amazing – the city of sails, with a stunning harbourside and proper 'new world' architecture (they have a huge tower in the centre of town and people can leap off it on a bungee cord). It was different to anything I had ever experienced – I even watched people get out of cars in their bare feet and walk into the bank, which was just brilliant, you don't get that in Buchanan Street. And the main street, Queen Street, was nothing like its Glaswegian namesake. It sprawled right across the city, on a hill, and was covered with so many fabulous shops and gorgeous restaurants.

I was booked into the same hotel as the other comics brought over from UK (all male – what a shock). There was a slightly awkward tension with some of them. A few wanted to know who 'brought me over'. I think I was the first female Scottish comic to attend the festival, and I wasn't 'brought over', which is when a promoter pays for all your expenses and gives you a set wage. I explained that I was funding this trip myself, and they were pretty cool about it.

The comedy circuit in New Zealand is surprisingly similar to the Scottish circuit; because it's smaller and has fewer clubs the local comics have to work that much harder. Even their open-spot new acts were bloody amazing and could easily hold their own with the experienced international guests.

The other comics were all playing at Auckland's main comedy venue and I was in a wee pub up the road called the Temple. I was sharing a stage in the window of the bar with Bret and Jermaine from *Flight of the Conchords*. They would do my door and take the money, then get me onstage, and I would do the same for them. I had initially hoped I would at least make some cash from my performances, so I wasn't too out of pocket. But it was going even better than I could have hoped – we were selling out every night and I was getting good word of mouth. A Scottish woman hadn't been there to swear that loudly EVER!

The local comics and the amazing women who were running the festival – a hearty bunch headed by Hilary Coe and her team – embraced me as one of their own and made me feel incredibly welcome. It genuinely was so different from Edinburgh or Glasgow comedy festivals.

I had the best time ever; I was picking up extra gigs and even took the ferry to Waiheke Island to wander around. It was amazing. I loved that they embraced their Māori culture and that the place was so multicultured for such a small island. The food, oh my *God* the food was the best ever. I still dream of the chicken teriyaki at Tanuki's Cave.

New Zealand proved to me that I was not just a Scottish comic but an international one. That festival was a turning point for me; I felt as though I had passed a huge test by proving that Scottish comedy, and my accent, can travel.

6

AFTER SIX YEARS of shouting back at hecklers and taking on tough crowds, my strong and fearless approach and penchant for swearing were annoying some of the male comics. I was asked by a few of the guys backstage in different big chain clubs to be 'more gentle' and 'less aggressive when I MC'. So, for a while, wherever and whenever I was performing, I toned 'loud Janey' down to be more 'amenable'. I imagined I was wearing a good underskirt and baking nice buns for the boys. Only this meant that by the time the other comics went onstage in the bigger Jongleurs comedy nights, the crowd was pretty unmanageable – lots of drunks shouting and people just ignoring the stage. So then one of the management team would take me aside and ask me to do my job and 'control them'. I couldn't win.

Swearing had been a big part of my act since I started. But swearing was, and still is, an irritating issue for women in comedy in the UK.

Picture the scene. I walk out of a gig at the Edinburgh Fringe, it's raining. I'm laughing and saying goodbye to some folks before I get straight into a cab and someone shouts, 'Loved the show Janey!'

'Are you a comedian?' asks the taxi driver, looking at me in the rear-view mirror.

'Yes I am,' I reply quite proudly, forgetting, in my elation, that I usually don't speak about comedy in taxis. I know exactly what he is going to say next, but before I can think of a diversion, I hear him ask the inevitable question: 'Do you swear?'

I have my stock answer: 'I don't swear any more than the male comics or less than the local priest.' That usually makes them look into their mirror, disapprovingly. Then I hear him say, 'Ah, you're one of those feminist women . . .' as if the only way I could possibly answer them back is because I have a political agenda and some buckwheat sandals that I wear as I breastfeed foundlings on my lactating pendulous braless titties.

'No more a feminist than most of the male comics but usually more than the local priest. Have you ever asked a male comic if he swears?' I add, hoping this will end this painfully awkward corner we have talked our way into.

I don't listen to his response, I just pull on my headphones (always a great way to get out of such situations) and nod to music as he mouths some shit I cannot hear while his eyebrows look knotted and angry.

I don't know why 'swearing' is something that females have to be told not to do. Is it really that bad? Has anyone ever really hated Kevin Bridges', Frankie Boyle's or Billy Connolly's language onstage to the point where they discuss it with a pursed mouth?

When Dara Ó Briain says the word 'Feck' live on television, we all know it means 'fuck'. Does Dara get belittled for being an uneducated, ill-informed swearer? No, he doesn't. He is known for being one of Ireland's most intelligently funny men.

So, is it a class issue? I have seen very well-spoken, middle-class English women swear in comedy and somehow it is more acceptable, especially if said by an 'apparent slip of the tongue' or via the medium of a 'puppet' (see Nina Conti's filthy-mouthed Monkey).

Does my swearing sound worse because I am a working-class Scottish woman?

If I was an Oxbridge graduate, wearing a tea dress and swearing onstage, would it be seen as 'edgy and gritty', like a hipster getting angry at a flat tyre? In my East End accent, does it instead sound really harsh and filthy and all you hear is a slovenly washerwoman taking us back years with her filthy language?

Who knows? I bought a house by swearing. I am not changing now.

When it comes to shouting back, it goes deeper than just a penchant for bad language. Through recent therapy, I have realised that as a result of my difficult childhood, and the trauma I suffered with the abuse, I was always fighting. And I just didn't know when to stop. That resilience I had as a child stayed with me. As I grew up, I was usually a lone woman in a male-dominated space, like in the pub and in comedy, so I felt I had to be tough to be able to stand up for myself. When I started out in comedy all those years ago, my first few gigs mainly consisted of me just screaming at the audience – I think I thought I was still behind the bar. I kept fighting all my life and, when I didn't have to fight any more, I think I didn't know how to stop. This was something that would continue on social media in years to come.

It's a tough tightrope to walk as a woman, to stand up for yourself without being labelled as 'aggressive' or 'too much'. On top of that, if I did better onstage than the guys they'd sometimes hit back at me with snarky remarks like, 'That crowd just wanted period jokes and women's shite.' It always felt like I was stealing their slice of the pie, as though there'd have been more for them if I hadn't been there.

In the early noughties, there was even a male comic who used to dress in a black curly wig and frock and run onstage shouting, 'I've been abused as a child!' as a cruel parody of me. I know this because my sister saw him do it. She said the other acts had a good laugh at me, too.

That said, the majority of the male comics I met were incredibly supportive and very protective of women on the bill. I know there are many female comics who have suffered sexual assault, rape, dick pics and a plethora of abuse from certain men in the industry, and comedy promoters protected them. That's a story for another day, and not my truth to tell. But when that day comes, we should all listen. It took years, and the internet, for women in comedy to have their #metoo moment – it should have happened sooner.

When I was starting out, it was pretty normalised for male comics to get naked onstage and make extremely lewd comments to women in the audience. I saw more cock in comedy than I ever saw at the most rowdy drunken nights in my pub.

One night at an outdoor gig in Perth in July, I sat in the crowd waiting to see a well-known Scottish comic headline the show. I'd done my ten minutes and it had gone down well; the audience was sun-soaked and cheery, slowly getting drunker. A couple of the other comics and I were lying on the grass and, when the headline act came on, the crowd roared and cheered. He grabbed a guitar and started singing in a wispy voice and immediately you could feel the atmosphere shift into this grumbling wave of annoyance. 'Tell us some jokes!' some guy shouted and at that the comedian stood up, got naked and started to ballet-dance around the stage, his floppy giblets dangling as he pranced and screamed at everyone. People started to leave the festival tent and I heard someone say, 'When he's good, he's genius but you have to catch him at the right time.'

You will never hear that about a female comic. Women don't get afforded such leeway. We have to get it right first time. And we'd be called everything under the sun for getting our fannies out. We wouldn't be called a genius that's for sure. Such is life.

In early 2001 I was running a comedy club in London's swanky Atlantic Bar near Piccadilly. It was the 'it' bar of the moment, full of the famous and fancy faces on the scene back then. It once attracted the likes of Robert De Niro, Madonna and Harvey Keitel and was considered the coolest place in town.

The bar was set in the basement of an old hotel at Piccadilly Circus and was a beautiful example of original art deco. The ornate winding staircase presented the glamorous and the good with an opportunity to glide into the place like a sultry sex siren from old Hollywood. I turned up in jeans and a sweatshirt doing comedy and booking acts. On Sundays we had the comedy gig in the side room called Dick's Bar. I loved it.

One afternoon after a meeting, I was sat at the bar having a cup of tea when a bunch of men in black coats came strolling in, all shifty eyes and shiny shoes. I recognised the type: old gangsters and young hangers-on. An elderly man came over to me at the bar and said, 'Excuse me, that's my seat.'

It wasn't his seat; I had been there for nearly an hour reading a book. I looked about the near-empty bar and said, 'I don't think so, go sit elsewhere.'

The men that flanked him – and surrounded me – all stood still and stared me down. The older man leaned over and said with a growl, 'I'm Mad Frankie Fraser.'

I looked him right in the eye and said, 'I don't care if you're mad Frankie Howerd, I am not getting off this fucking seat.'

He was silent for a second. Then he burst out laughing. We actually ended up having a good chat. My barmaid days have seen me through many a tight corner, and my Scottish accent usually breaks the ice – it has a 'fuck you' feel to it, which is helpful at times. It was only afterwards that I realised I had challenged one of the most notorious and dangerous men of London's criminal underworld. Woops.

Monica came with me every week to Dick's Bar, and we had some fabulous well-known acts as well as some brand-new comics onstage. It was our own wee comedy gang. I was in my element, picking up gigs before and after the show at the Atlantic, but all this work meant I was commuting to London every weekend.

The logistics were tough sometimes, going back and forth between two cities, trying to keep the costs down and make a living. Sean was getting fed up with the train prices, accommodation was getting to be a bigger financial burden – I didn't want to keep staying on a mate's couch, and hotels were extortionate – but mostly I missed Ashley.

Still, I was loving the gig, even if the Atlantic didn't pay enough. It was brilliant getting to spend so much time with Monica, too. She and I had the best fun ever back then. She was single, and I wasn't much help – despite my best efforts, my matchmaking skills were possibly the worst ever. Fair to say I never found her the man of her dreams. If it wasn't baldy-headed, loud Essex boys I was introducing her to, it was shy introverted comedians who couldn't cope with her big personality. Now we look back and howl with laughter at my failed attempts.

'You don't get to pick me a man,' Monica once told me in between fits of laughter. 'What do you know about adult relationships? You got married so young you got Kerplunk as a wedding present.' I laughed along, but she was right. My marriage had been through the wars and it wasn't in the best place. My regular travelling for the best part of five years had been hard enough to deal with already, and practically living in London for half the week wasn't making things any easier.

Getting on trains or planes every weekend, living in hotels or with mates as Ashley was left to deal with life without me, wasn't ideal. Her dad was either deeply depressed or just managing to hang on and be present for her. Mentally, he was scraping by. He assured me that I had to make decisions that were right for my job but, at the same time, he was throwing moods that made me hesitate leaving Ashley alone with him.

I felt as though I was abandoning my responsibilities. I regret leaving so much, and I accept that I should have done better and tried to stay in Glasgow more, but comedy isn't that kind of job. I was getting more work, yes, but I still wasn't at the stage of being able to pick and choose where and when I performed. I had to take any jobs I could, and the club in London was only temporary anyway.

It was my choice to do this job. I picked the one career that was evidently not made for women, especially not a middle-aged woman, *especially* not a working-class Scottish woman. I genuinely couldn't have picked a harder career in the mid-nineties. But I couldn't have done anything else.

7

As TIME WENT on, it was becoming more obvious that it wasn't just depression that Sean was dealing with. His behaviour was sometimes completely erratic and unfathomable to outsiders. It was no help that I had been used to his mood swings and odd obsessive periods and was basically facilitating them. It was only when Ashley came across an article about Asperger's and autism online that something clicked for us. We were both astounded by the similarities between his behaviour and the points made in the journal. We openly discussed this with Sean, who was baffled by the whole thing. 'Are you sure I'm not just an evil bastard?' he asked.

When we went through all the behavioural aspects, he was pretty convinced we were right and he started getting help with a psychologist.

It didn't make life easier, and it didn't really change things – we still had many years of his tantrums and obsessive behaviour to come – but at least Sean had someone else to talk to, and now we all had some clarity. We finally understood why he couldn't stand sudden loud noises or why he freaked out if we got upset at something, or why he would rant for hours about some stupid unimportant subject that I had to listen to and pretend to be interested in.

I had spent so much of my life appeasing him to stop him getting into a state about something that didn't really matter, like a mistake I made in an email, or if I misunderstood a conversation. It could be anything. He would routinely point out any mistakes I made and obsess about them, but if he made a mistake or had an accident of some sort it wasn't to be mentioned.

Sean had been living in a state of fear and guilt ever since trusting his family and losing everything, which was his 'mistake', he thought. He kept telling me he ruined everything. He was never at peace. Through his therapy we got to discuss 'mistakes' and how to react to them. To this day he still has problems admitting a mistake and still has to be told to shut up when he points out mine.

My husband was different from every other man I'd ever known in my life. Yes, he had a lot of temper problems. I sometimes look back on the marriage and wonder, what the fuck was I doing? He was difficult a lot of the time, but when he was good he was brilliant, and when he was kind he was incredibly kind. He would do anything for Ashley, he would even lend money to my friends if they needed it. Most importantly, he would always be there for us when we needed him. That's what made me realise I had married the right man. He might not always have been the best husband, but he was the definitely the most caring person, and the best dad to Ashley.

Despite the tension in our marriage, Sean remained one of my biggest supporters. It was Sean who encouraged me to take the next big leap in my career, one that would bring me closer to my childhood dream.

I was a Fringe regular in the early noughties, and in between hundreds of comedy gigs – performing my own and watching others – I saw a lot of plays, too. And some of them were just so *shit*. After watching a particularly dreadful one, I said, 'I could do better.' Sean said, 'Do it then.' I did.

There was a new venue called the Underbelly down on the Cowgate, where I did a few stand-up slots in 2002. The guys there, Charlie and Ed, had been so supportive of my comedy. I was well used to making people laugh by then, but I knew I wanted to do something different. I wanted to write something that wasn't comedy.

My life back at the pub in The Calton was absolutely defined by the flood of heroin that had arrived in the city. As a community, we saw young people die one after the other. Parents were waking up to dead kids and they had nowhere to turn. They had just survived the glue-sniffing epidemic and now they were facing their teens burning heroin in their bedrooms. So many young people lost their lives, and their parents had no idea what was killing them. You have to think of the time; it was 1979, nobody really knew what heroin was or what it was capable of doing – I'm talking about normal, everyday people, not rock stars and celebrities.

The epidemic hit my own family hard – my eldest brother Jim struggled with heroin addiction for years, and I lost my beloved cousin Sammy to the drug in the year 2000. I knew, first hand, the destruction that followed heroin.

I knew that this was what I had to write about. I wanted people to see the havoc caused by this plague that rampaged through Glasgow, how it affected the community I lived in, as well as the resilience of the families ripped apart by it. I wrote the play in six months and called it *The Point of Yes*. It was semi-autobiographical, based on all the stories and experiences from my Weavers Inn days.

I got a director called Graham, whom I met through Claire McCauley, the comedy promoter, and we both worked so hard to get the play into shape for August 2003. We were putting it on in the afternoons, at the same venue where I would be doing my comedy show in the evenings. I played the two characters in the play, so it was all down to me. There was Janey who ran a pub and an imaginary Janey who left the pub and ended up on drugs.

Sean, Ashley and I were staying in a wee, ancient flat down on the Grassmarket in Edinburgh. It was eighty-seven steps up to the front door. I don't know how we managed every day traipsing up and down to do comedy shows and plays and other gigs in between. It was exhausting but great fun.

It was so brilliant to have Ashley there with me. She was my absolute rock at this point – she's always been my fiercest critic and biggest supporter. She produced the shows and did all the marketing and promotion – she was a flyering pro, so much so that she flyered for other acts and organised entire flyering teams. She was making more money than her dad and I were! She worked hard to get an audience in every night, and at the same time she was studying even harder for her Highers at school. At this point, Sean was also studying; he had started taking a college course on social studies.

It was doing him good to have the chance to get an education when, like me, he had left school at sixteen with no qualifications.

I was proud of what we had created, but the opening day was petrifying. I kept thinking, what if I couldn't act in front of an audience? And the play itself was so out of my comfort zone. I had written in small moments of comic relief, but on the whole it was quite a dark piece, so it was a real change from the sort of performances I was used to. Would people even like it? What if audiences came expecting a laugh and ended up depressed instead? Then the thought of sticking to a script was making me feel ill, too – I was so used to improvising in my gigs. What if I messed up my lines?

Thankfully, Sean and Ashley had every faith in me, and their support made me feel able to get up there and perform every day. What they did not have faith in, though, was the performance space, which was windowless, damp and smelled of death.

'This venue feels really creepy . . .' Ashley said to me when we first arrived the day before the first show, after we'd stumbled over wet cobblestones and up the steps to the main door of the building. The place was a giant four or five storeys high – depending on whether you viewed it from the front or the back – that stretched from Victoria Street down to the Cowgate in the old bit of town.

Parts of it were 800 years old – it was more ancient monument than theatre spot. Rumours that it had housed the dead during a plague didn't do it any favours, but a venue is a venue when it comes to the Fringe, so up we went, navigating the cobbles with boxes filled with props and hearts filled with hope and excitement.

Inside, the timeworn walls had red rusty liquid running down the internal bricks, like they were bleeding slowly from the inside. (That week at a photo shoot a huge boulder unhinged itself and almost killed Charlie Wood, the wonderful custodian of the venue – it was as if the building didn't like being disturbed.)

When we arrived, the techies explained how the day before they had wired the performance spaces and secured said wires with gaffer tape, yet this morning – after the place had lain empty overnight – it seemed all the tape had been violently ripped up. Nobody could explain it. We all carried on and giggled about the 'apparent haunting'; it gave the venue some character.

All year the place had lain dark and empty, and now it was full of fairy lights, wannabe actors and lighting rigs. It was like an old whore being dressed up for a bad wedding and it wasn't ready to give in without a fight.

Ashley and I walked through the myriad of rusted damp-smelling archways and found our room. Posters of comedians, actors and shows festooned the walls, but somehow they kept slowly peeling off, as if the building was shrugging off this forced shroud of happiness, hating the thought of having its crusty veneer touched.

Nothing felt right. The atmosphere in every room prickled the hairs on the back of your arms and, no matter how many times you walked into a space, the soil (yes, some rooms had a soil floor) beneath your feet somehow always shifted. Stages sat at a slight tilt, despite repeated repairs. Even the chairs creaked and moaned as you walked through our performance room.

There were about eight or nine performance spaces in the ancient building. I had one long room for my play. There was no backstage area, just a big, thick, black, damp – everything was permanently damp – curtain that ran in front of one of the decrepit walls that leaked the red, sticky rusty stuff that no one was able to explain. I had to stand behind that curtain every day in the windowless, airless room in the pitch black.

I hated those three minutes standing with my face near a weeping wall that was hundreds of years old while I waited for the stage lights to go up. It was unsettling, to say the least.

Thankfully, the play was a huge success, despite doors constantly falling off their frames in the room, the floor making a noise that nobody could trace and the chairs creaking through the quiet parts of the show. According to critics, my play was 'deeply moving'. Creepy venue aside, I was having the time of my life.

Until one stifling, damp afternoon, which will stay with me for ever.

8

IT WAS A particularly hot, sticky Fringe. Well, it always felt hot and sticky in the Underbelly venue and, as I was doing a play and then a comedy show at night, I don't think I left the place much.

That one afternoon, my tech, Gary, gave me the thumbs-up, and I took my place behind the curtain. As usual, I faced the wall, smelled the wet, sour wall-ooze and closed my eyes. The stage went dark and the soft house lights went up. I could hear the audience come in. The chairs creaked, the room moaned, and I concentrated on my first lines. I had a whole hour of pretty harrowing, difficult dialogue to get through, and I was determined to do a good job.

We were getting near lights up and the room had plunged into a thick, hard darkness when I felt this strange, tickling, prickling feeling on my bare arms. I frantically brushed them down, worried an insect had landed on me (oh yes, did I mention the tiny wee flying things that occupied the place? No?).

So I waited and rubbed my arms. This was taking too long. Where was the stage light? Why were the house lights down? What was happening? We didn't have a system where I could be told if there was any delay. I assumed it was just front of house letting latecomers in.

Then, in the pitch darkness behind the curtain, right beside me, I heard a voice whisper, 'Hey . . . Janey.'

I thought the staff were trying to get my attention, so I turned my head towards it and there in the velvety darkness was a pale face near mine.

A face I didn't recognise. I gulped and stared.

My heart was already pounding with pre-show nerves and adrenalin pumping through my veins. I couldn't think straight. Was this the Dutch girl who was front of house? I couldn't tell.

I leaned towards the face and said, 'What is it?'

Nothing happened. The face stayed there, it smiled. My pupils adjusted, shrank and focused. Everything was still. Time seemed suspended. It was an older face I had never seen before.

What was happening? Had I missed the cue lights? Where was the music I had organised to top the play? The face got close enough for me to feel an icy breath that was tinged with a stench of decay.

The hairs on my arms sprang up again. I caught my breath. My legs felt like lead and all the blood in my body rushed to my heart.

The face quivered and then somehow floated against the wall, all the while maintaining eye contact with me.

What the fuck was going on? How could so many people be fifteen feet away from me and not know what was happening back here in the dark?

The face smiled at me, still staring, and I shivered again, so completely petrified that I almost cried out for help.

Then the hoarse voice whispered right at me. It said my name again: 'Janey . . .'

I froze on the spot, my body shook and I felt sick. Its face was clear but its body was formless and constantly shifting. I knew it wasn't human, it wasn't anything my brain could make sense of. Was the heat making me delirious?

As my brain tried to figure out what was happening, the face suddenly disappeared and the stage lights came up, the music started and it was time for me to get onstage.

I walked right through the space where that face had been and went on to shakily deliver my opening line. My mouth was dry, like I had swallowed a cup of sand, my brain was all over the place. How was I going to get through this whole hour?

I don't think I have ever performed that play with such a high level of adrenalin; my heart was pounding and I was totally aware of every single skin cell on my body.

I managed fine – somehow the words all came out. But I had to go backstage to change character with each scene.

Every time I had to walk back behind the curtain, even if just for a few seconds, I kept my head down and closed my eyes for fear that face would reappear.

It didn't. Or at least I don't know if it did – my eyes were shut tight and I couldn't hear anything.

When the last line was delivered and I walked behind the curtain at the end of the show, I heard the audience leave the room. I looked around behind the curtain, I searched the sticky wall with my eyes wide and mouth agape.

I jumped when I heard the staff shout, 'Show done, well done guys!'

The place fell silent and I walked out onto the stage and shouted to my techie, 'Gary, I heard a weird whisper before we opened, did the staff come behind the curtain? What happened to the music and the lights at the top of the show?'

'Sorry, Janey, but just before we opened I couldn't get the lights or music to work and there was a slight delay, that's why we started a few minutes late, sorry!' he shouted from the back of the room. 'I'll check the desk just now and figure out what went wrong.'

I was simultaneously terrified and confused; I couldn't work out what the hell had just happened. In a daze, I began to pack up the props as the next show came in.

We never found out what happened. I didn't see that face or hear that spine-chilling whisper for the rest of the run.

That was until the last night of the Fringe. The shows were all done, the building was slowly being stripped of posters and lighting rigs, the performers were all gathering their props and getting ready to party their last night away.

I suppose I kind of forgot about the face behind the curtain.

I went back into my empty performance space for one last look around. I was full of emotion, glad and so proud to have performed the first play that I had ever written. With a satisfied sigh, I headed in to clear out my props, which were in the room next door to the stage.

It's quite poignant leaving a place after the intensity of performing there every day for a month. There's an energy you leave behind. I can't explain it.

The walls still leaked, the room still felt damp and the thick and dusty dirt shifted beneath my shoes. As I stood there, alone, packing up my stuff, I heard a whisper behind me.

I turned round with a start. I scanned the small room, but there was nothing there, just the jumbled boxes of props, old army uniforms, chairs, a big papier mâché owl and clothes strewn beneath a costume rack.

My nerves started to kick in again. I could feel my mouth go dry.

I tentatively walked towards the theatre space and creaked open the stage door. It was pitch dark in there with only the light from the props room throwing a shaft onto the floor.

I could hear the pounding music from the bar downstairs.

'Is anyone in here?' I shouted.

Nothing, there was no reply, just dense darkness.

As I moved to close the door and walk back into the light of the props room, I heard another faint whisper, but I couldn't make out what it was. Fear gripped me, my insides ran completely cold, my legs felt watery and I could hear my heart banging like a jackhammer in my ears.

I went against all my instincts, threw out a shaky hand and pushed the theatre door wide open and let the dim light behind me flood the room.

There was nothing there but faint dust motes dancing through the thick air, then something grabbed me from behind, a cold hand yanked me backwards. I think the utter shock made my heart stop. I felt faint and screamed as loud as I have ever done in my entire life.

'Calm down Mum, it's me, why are you screaming like that? Move it, this place scares me without you screaming like a banshee, get the props, Dad is waiting downstairs.'

Ashley stood there staring at me in shock.

As I let the stage door bang shut, somewhere from inside the room I heard faint voices fade away, and a blast of fetid air smacked me in the face.

I never looked back. We both headed down the back stairs, skittered over the damp cobbles and headed out of the venue.

Anyway, other than the scary voices and the haunted blood juice dripping down the walls, the play went well. It might sound strange given the tone of the piece, but it was just a joy to perform every day. The Underbelly staff were really supportive, helping to spread the word and making sure the shows ran smoothly. Every day I got bigger and bigger audiences and it even got a great review from the *Scotsman* theatre reviewer Joyce McMillan. I was over the moon that I had written something and acted it so well that people were enjoying it. I'd *finally* got to be the actor I always wanted to be. Not bad for a girl with no O-levels to her name.

Towards the end of the run, a man called John Fleming came to see both the play and my comedy show that followed in the evening, and spoke to me afterwards over a coffee in the Underbelly cafe. We had many mutual comedy friends – John was a middle-aged comedy geek. But he had also worked as a researcher in telly and had connections in the publishing world.

I thought he just wanted to chat about the show, but he had something else in mind.

'You should write a book,' he told me. 'Your story is incredible, it should be heard.'

9

I HAD ALWAYS thought about writing it all down, the story of my childhood, just to sort it out in my head and make sense of it all. It had been suggested to me before, but I was still gobsmacked when John said it – I almost choked on the mediocre coffee I was drinking. I never really believed it could be an actual thing I would do.

John had helped write *I Stole Freddie Mercury's Birthday Cake*, the autobiography of the late godfather of alternative comedy, Malcolm Hardee, so he knew what he was doing – and he had the connections to help me. He encouraged me to start writing a blog, which helped me pull childhood memories out from deep inside my brain. Once writing was under way, John contacted a publisher he knew at Ebury, part of the Random House group. I was thrilled to hear he was keen to meet me. We had some very productive meetings, but even so I still didn't believe anything was actually going to come of it.

Then, a few weeks later, I opened an email from Ebury offering me a book deal. I sat there blinking at the computer screen for a minute, before going to the bathroom to sit on the loo and quietly weep. Never in a thousand million years did I think something like this would happen to someone like me.

My family were so proud of me, my dad was so chuffed: 'You'll be great at this Janey, let them all know the truth,' he said with a gleam in his eye. Monica was so excited: 'You're a brilliant storyteller, you can do it!' she said.

I was going to write a book about all the mental shit that had happened to me when I was younger, and I was looking forward to sharing the funny moments and the sad. I knew it was going to be painful, but I hoped finally telling the whole story would be a cathartic experience too. Even better, I would finally have a decent pay cheque to help out the family. It was all thanks to John and the confidence he gave me to write it all down.

The next step was to find an agent to get the deal done for me. I recall walking around Soho, just looking for a door that said 'literary agent'. No luck. I stopped for coffee and remembered that Charlie from the Underbelly had a relative in publishing. I called him straight away from the cafe and he directed me to his Aunt Amanda in nearby Berwick Street. Relief. Now I had an agent, as well as a publisher, and almost a contract. So all I had to do was write the book.

I told Sean that I wouldn't be whitewashing anything, I would tell the truth about what we had been through together. He never once told me what not to write but I do know to this day he's never read my first book; nor has Ashley.

John helped me enormously. In our first meeting after the deal, he sat me down in Bar Italia in Soho and said, 'Get all the chapters in order and then start writing the way you speak.' It sounded too simple. I was petrified – how the fuck do I write a book?

I started with the basics – I bought a good laptop and taught myself how to type. All those years at school when I refused to sit in secretarial class had come back to bite me – I had so much to learn. I tried to spend any free time I had writing. I sat in hotels and wrote when I was on tour, furiously jabbing at the keys on my laptop.

I'm a big reader myself; books have always been my way of escaping my often-difficult reality. I thought this would help me when it came to writing one of my own, but it was tough going. It was difficult enough mastering the tech, figuring out how to save the documents and not lose them. Writing a book was so different from writing a play, and I had never written my comedy material down – I just kept it all in my head – so I was a bag of nerves. I didn't know if I could do it at all. Everything was going to have to be put down chronologically, with proper grammar, a story arc and lots of typing, all of which I wasn't sure I could do.

If I ever had writer's block, or didn't know how to get the right words out, John would just make me talk about things that had happened in my life, and then say, 'Ok, just write that bit down like that.' I knew I wanted to include lots of funny stories along with the dark ones – it was important to get the balance right.

I also knew it had to be honest. It was painful writing about how my mum knew I was being abused but didn't rescue me from her brother. And it was difficult reliving all the sexual abuse and finding a way to write it without completely horrifying the reader. When I was back home, I wrote during the night so my family wouldn't see me getting upset as I struggled through the tough bits.

After months working as a circuit comic, being a mum, trying to keep my marriage in good health, and travelling up and down the country, I finally managed to finish *Handstands in the Dark*. I was so nervous sending the final draft to the publisher, in case it was just a big pile of jumbled words and nonsense. But they loved it, thank God.

If only I could have taken a minute to breathe and wait for my book to be published. But I had to focus on getting back to the Fringe. Thankfully, I had my daughter on hand to help.

Ashley had turned eighteen; she had finished school, and was heading for university in September – where does the time go, I asked myself. She spent most of her summer working at one of her temporary jobs (secretary, care worker, shop assistant and even DJ); she was really grafting to earn her own cash before coming to Edinburgh in August to help me with my shows. I genuinely couldn't have done it without her.

Ashley wasn't the only help at the Fringe that year. My best pal Monica had introduced me to her sister, Elaine, and her wee lassie Gabrielle, who although just four was a dab hand at flyering under Ashley's watchful eye. They can't start too young! And by the time she was eighteen, Gabby had become head of my flyering team at the Fringe – it's a family circus when the Fringe comes round.

Good Godley! was the show I took to the Fringe that year. It built on everything I'd finally managed to come to terms with through writing my book. It exposed all the stories about the child abuse, the violence and my mum's murder. Yes, it was shocking but it was also a comedy show and really full of belly laughs. It was great to finally laugh at the darkest shit in my life and see other people join in.

The show opened back at the Underbelly and within days the whole run had sold out. I went from having no reviews to gathering 5-star reviews almost daily. And I couldn't believe there were queues of people lining up to see me. The middle-aged woman making funny stories about rape and murder. I think I was at the forefront of 'confessional comedy' in 2004.

I really felt that I had been vindicated. Too many times I'd been put down by local club owners who'd never thought I'd amount to anything – now I was even being tipped for the Perrier comedy award. Though that didn't stop one club owner sneering, 'I don't care if you win the Perrier, you won't get a gig at the Stand.' Which wasn't very insightful, seeing as I'd been barred from there for years.

The joke's on him anyway, because I did – eventually – get a gig at the Stand. It took a few years, but I got there. So this is my Alan Partridge moment to say, 'They were wrong and I was right!'

I may not have won the Perrier – apparently my problem was that I improvised too much, instead of saying the same thing night after night – but I was finally being recognised as a comic in other ways. I was asked to film a TV show on Channel 4 called *Kings of Comedy*, which was a *Big Brother*-style reality show where older comics went up against younger comics (thankfully we got out at weekends to do our gigs). This was huge for me; my nerves were through the roof. The money wasn't great, and the show had a very weird format, but I was going to be doing stand-up on Channel 4!

In the end, I'm afraid my appearance on that show would be remembered for another reason. There was another female comic on with me who used the word 'cunt' live on telly, and so naturally viewers complained. But in the press, Ofcom reported that it was me who had uttered it and demanded I make an apology. How ironic then that they had to apologise for just assuming it was my fault. But that was life, eh? Working-class voices always seemed to get the blame for the bad words. Of course, I did use that word very publicly, years later, but we will get to that.

Kings of Comedy didn't make it past one series, but my career was going from strength to strength nonetheless – my play *The Point of Yes*, which I had debuted at the Fringe two years before, went to London's Soho Theatre.

89

I couldn't believe it. It was surreal enough to perform in the Fringe, never mind Theatreland. I had walked past the Soho Theatre so many times, and now my face was on posters in the window. After the first few performances, people started to look at me differently. It was as if I was finally accepted. I was an actor, I was good and I now had a critically acclaimed show of my own at the famous Soho Theatre. This was huge.

The Soho Theatre had an arrangement with the Groucho Club – the exclusive celebrity haunt down the street – which meant people performing there could get access to the club.

I remember the first time going in with Ashley, I was incredibly nervous and convinced the bouncers would throw us out. Behind the reception was a wee guy in a flamboyant tiger-print coat and long wavy hair called Bernie. I explained I was on at the Soho Theatre, and he demanded I do a bit of the play right there in reception. I thought this was how they weeded out the liars, so, in front of a few startled guests getting their coats off I performed the part of Act Two where I talk about injecting heroin into my leg. Bernie clapped his hands in delight and waved us through.

Ashley and I tentatively picked our way through the fancy bar, spotting a few well-known faces on the way, but we were determined to play it cool and not make eye contact. Later I did do that awful thing though where I saw a woman in the toilet and thinking it was someone I knew said, 'Oh hello, how are you?' and when she didn't answer I followed up with, 'It's me, Janey.' She was a famous actor, but my brain told me, 'There's your pal.' I was so embarrassed but thankfully she was really kind about it and laughed it off. It was just like the time I saw a man I recognised in the queue for a flight and said, 'You're a comedian, aren't you?' before Ashley dragged me away and said, 'That's Noel Gallagher!' I am such a dick.

The Groucho Club was fabulous. We met the manageress, who was a wee curvy red-haired belter of a woman called June, and of course she was Scottish too. She introduced me to so many cool people and invited me to perform at the Gang Show, which is an event that raises thousands of pounds for charity and also means you get to perform with some of the biggest names in music and theatre. Also it comes with a year's membership, which felt like getting the Willy Wonka Golden Ticket to social-circle paradise! How I loved pushing through the paparazzi and getting through those brass-framed doors in Dean Street. Stand back boys, I have arrived!

I became a Groucho regular and I am sworn to secrecy about everything I saw in there, cos that's the rules.

It might sound cheesy to say, but I really did feel like I had made it. Especially when *Handstands in the Dark* came out the same month that my play ran at Soho Theatre. I had gone from being a circuit comic to a playwright, actor and now published author.

I will never forget the thrill of holding the hardback in my hands for the first time. I actually sobbed when it came through the door. I took it up to my dad as soon as it arrived, and he cried almost as much as I had. It was such a touching moment between us; Dad and I were very close and he knew how much this meant to me. He ordered heaps of copies of the book and gave them out to everyone he met, even strangers on the bus.

I know Ashley was proud of me too. As she grew older, she began to understand that, despite all my absences as a mum, I loved what I did – comedy, acting, writing, getting to be creative. She'd accepted it, but the guilt didn't leave me. I don't think it ever will. It's still hard to think she had to be a carer for her dad through his emotional breakdowns. That wasn't her role to play.

When *Handstands in the Dark* came out in 2005 it quickly became a bestseller. It received so many great reviews – people even wrote to me to tell me about their own personal stories of abuse and overcoming adversity. The book made me feel as though I had really lived. People who knew me well knew most of the story, but even they were still a bit taken aback by all I had gone through. I had spent so many years feeling ashamed of my childhood. Now, here I was feeling proud that I had been able to tell my story.

10

THE BOOK WAS now giving me a wider audience and I knew I should try to capitalise on that, but I didn't know how – I didn't have a comedy agent or someone to push me forward or help plan my career. Although even under my own steam, I felt like I was breaking ground as a female comic.

I was delighted that Ashley had reached the age where we could reap the rewards of all our hard work together. That summer, she and I went to Glastonbury as I was one of the first females to host the comedy tent. I had gone to Glastonbury for the first time the year before by myself to do stand-up. Of course, it rained like a tropical storm, and staying in a wee damp tent and squishing about in wellies almost drove me insane. Lots of middle-class folk like roughing it in the muck, but I'd lived in poverty and dirt and somehow this just triggered me no end. But I can't say I didn't have a good time; standing onstage in front of thousands of people making them laugh was just brilliant. Sleeping in a tent with a wet clock beetle next to my face and having a period in a temporary toilet cabin, not so much.

This year, I was very honoured and equally scared to MC, as it's not an easy crowd to contain and I didn't want to fuck it up. When one woman fucks up a gig in comedy, all the women are tarred with the same brush. But men can fuck up and they don't assume all other men will be shit. It's a big responsibility.

And there was another stress factor for me. The late Malcom Hardee, a comedy agent and comedian himself, known for his outrageous stunts, had died that year in a tragic drowning accident in Rotherhithe. It was he who had given me the chance to perform at Glastonbury and he was very much missed by all the performers. I knew I had a lot to live up to.

Ashley was super excited. She LOVED running about in wellies, getting backstage with VIP passes, and mixing with all the young people who were part of the families working backstage. There was, unsurprisingly, torrential rain that year too. This time, it caused biblical floods and one night the wee bridge over the stream collapsed. I heard someone shout, 'The stream has overflowed and that Scottish lass is in there helping people out!' I dropped the cup I was drinking out of, pushed a rubber boat aside and waded through the catering tent, up to my armpits in water. Panic burned in my chest as I fought to get through the mud and high rain floods, to find Ashley stood in the stream passing people arm to arm. 'Get the fuck *out* of there!' I screamed. 'There are big men standing around, they can go in!' I was absolutely petrified she'd drown just like my mammy did. But Ashley ignored me and carried on. Then, completely unfazed, she climbed out and headed through the mud for the showers.

Later, I watched her sitting round the bonfire drinking out of a champagne bottle with Arabella Churchill. Yes, Winston's granddaughter. I still can see them laughing and chatting away together. Arabella was a wonderful woman and a huge supporter of Glastonbury and many worthy charities. She sadly passed away only a year later.

It felt surreal to think about how far I had come from my own childhood to now raising a daughter and having her watch me perform at Glastonbury.

After a brilliantly busy couple of years without a pause, I thought I'd treat myself to a wee holiday on my own. This was the first time I had gone alone for leisure and not work. I chose to go to Rome. It was . . . interesting. Not only did I get a facial in a beauty salon where the woman accidentally electrocuted my face with two fancy skin-smoothing probes, but I fell flat on my face in the street outside the Vatican and a nun stood on my fingers.

Seeing as the holiday was a failed attempt at R&R, I was glad to get back to work, which meant heading back to the New Zealand Comedy Festival – this time with Ashley in tow. I was so excited to introduce her to all my friends and show her the amazing places I had performed the last time I was there.

The last time I'd been in New Zealand, I was doing comedy in a pub, then a basement, basically an unknown; now I was being brought over with all expenses paid. I was a playwright, actor, published author – and now a BBC radio host too! A few months before, I had been asked by the late great Ned Sherrin to work on BBC Radio 4's show *Loose Ends*. Ned was a great champion for me. He not only had me as a guest on the show, but also had me write for and interview people on his very popular celebrity slot.

So here I was preparing to tour New Zealand with my daughter. Just a few years before, I couldn't have imagined that Ashley and I would be arriving in Auckland in style, not just begging for a minuscule slot on their festival.

Ashley's usually a great travel companion but we landed at 4 a.m. and she hadn't eaten on the plane since the stopover in LA, so she was hyper exhausted and hangry. We checked into the Heritage Hotel – where I had stayed on my first visit – and I had hoped to go to bed, but Ashley wouldn't sleep. 'Mum, when does breakfast start? I'm starving,' she cried. The hotel buffet wasn't open yet, so she was raiding my carry-on luggage bag, shouting, 'You must have at least a biscuit or *something* in your fucking bag!' I thought I was going to have to breastfeed her. We went down to the restaurant and waited for the place to open. When it did, Ashley raided the bread basket and had the toaster going as soon as it was turned on.

Once Ashley overcame her 'hanger', we had the best time together in New Zealand. We flew down to Wellington as the tour continued and both of us were screaming blue murder when the plane landed like a drop zone because the runway was so short.

We may have been off to a bumpy start, but the gigs in Wellington went fabulously well. I had a slot on the New Zealand Comedy Festival Gala, which is their big Saturday-night TV show, and I know Ashley was super chuffed to see her mum up there on the big stage. It was just a brilliant time travelling and gigging with her by my side. Over the years, doing stand-up has taken me – and Ashley – all across the country, and all around the world. I have done gigs in Atlanta, Spain, Germany,

Kuala Lumpur, Australia, the Netherlands, Boston and Los Angeles. I still pinch myself that work for me means getting to travel the world.

By this stage in my career, I was also performing all over the UK for Jongleurs comedy club and finally getting work at the Stand comedy clubs in both Edinburgh and Glasgow.

I mostly went to gigs up and down the country by train or plane, alone, which I didn't mind. If anything, travelling to gigs actually provided me with a lot of comedy material. One of my favourite stories, amongst many I may add, is this one about a night I was gigging in Oxford.

I was heading to Oxford by train, changing at Banbury rail station. Sitting in Banbury station, I started to munch into a big bag of crisps. They were particularly yummy as I hadn't eaten all day.

I noticed a middle-aged grey-haired man sitting beside me in the station concourse staring at me.

'You will spoil your tea eating them,' he said in a Glasgow accent. I just smiled and carried on eating – the last thing I wanted was to do was chat – but he seemed insistent on a conversation. As soon as he heard my accent he chipped, 'Where are you from in Glasgow?'

So, I filled him in quickly and explained that I was a comedian et cetera. He went quiet and listened as I told him that I travelled the world doing my job and that's why I was sitting in Banbury station.

He looked straight at me, his old Glaswegian teeth crookedly smiling as he asked, in all seriousness, 'Does your husband let you do this?'

I just stared at him and took a breath while about eighty million images flashed through my head, scenarios where I am in a crinoline dress, batting a fan and begging my husband's permission for me to go to a hat shop without an escort. I laughed out loud and couldn't even begin to explain the dynamics of my life, and why should I? Then over the intercom came the announcement that my train to Oxford would be delayed, with no estimate on when it would arrive.

I immediately got up and headed for the information desk. After realising that there was no other way to go, I stood amongst about seventy-nine people and said loudly, 'Does anyone want to taxi-share to Oxford?'

A young guy with dark hair and headphones piped up, 'Yep, I'm in,' and a well-dressed, quite distinguished-looking man in a suit came forward and said he was in, too. So a bunch of strangers turned taxi chums headed for the exit of Banbury station.

We got in the car, figured out the price that we had to split between us all and belted up. I sat quiet in the cab, still laughing to myself that there were still men who thought my husband 'allowed' me to work in a job that I created for myself and I am good at.

Just then the distinguished-looking man in the front seat turned round to me and said in a really lovely posh accent, 'I know you; I have seen your show at Edinburgh.'

The dark-haired guy sitting beside me looked at me full on and I smiled at the front-seat man and said, 'Really?'

'Yes, you are Janey Godley; I am Ed Bartlam's dad.'

I gasped and laughed out loud. Ed Bartlam – a wonderful, posh English guy whom I love – is the co-owner of the Underbelly venue at the Edinburgh Fringe, where I had been performing for the last four years and where I would be performing two of my three shows that year.

I spotted my chance and quickly said to Mr Bartlam Senior, 'Give me your mobile phone, please!'

He looked at me, hesitated, and then passed his phone over. Scanning his address book and seeing Ed's number; I pressed call and waited as it rang out.

'Hello, Dad,' Ed said.

I spoke slowly and clearly. 'You are probably wondering why a woman is on your dad's mobile, aren't you, Ed?'

'Janey Godley, is that you?' Ed sounded surprised, but recognised my voice.

'Yes, it is – now listen up you wee posh fucker, I have your dad in a fast-moving car in Oxford, and we are going to harm him unless you agree to let me perform at the venue this year for free,' I shouted.

Ed went quiet. I think he was in shock. 'Why are you with my dad?' he muttered.

'I told you, it took me ages to work out his movements and now I have him, so if you want to see him alive, agree,' I snapped back. I took a picture of Mr Bartlam Senior and sent it to Ed by text. I handed the phone to the now laughing but pretending to be scared Mr Bartlam Senior.

'Hi Ed, Janey is right. They have me hostage, so just agree,' he urged.

I took the phone back and listened to Ed agree to my hostage terms.

Mr Bartlam Senior and I laughed our heads off.

We did eventually explain to Ed the whole coincidence of us both being together, and I jokingly told him I would hold him to the agreements. For a while it looked like I would have a cheap venue that year, with free food and drink for the whole run. Well, at least it gave me a funny story to tell onstage.

When the Fringe did come round that year I was busier than ever, doing three shows a day, one at the Assembly Rooms with *The Point of Yes* and then two at the Underbelly – a sketch show with Ashley and a new solo comedy show for me. It was exhausting but I loved the challenge.

11

TWELVE YEARS HAD passed since we left the pub and my husband's life had imploded. Our marriage had been put to the test, and it had survived. Thankfully, the progress I had made with my job and the financial security that came with it meant that our relationship was now on a much better footing. And thank God that it was, because difficult times were coming our way.

But first, good news – much to my amazement, my play *The Point of Yes* was heading to New York! Back when I debuted the play at the Fringe, a guy named Cal Wynter had come to see me perform. It turned out Cal ran some theatres in New York, and was scouring the Fringe for plays he liked to bring back to the States.

We chatted for a bit and then, as casual as anything, he said, 'You should bring that to my theatre in Bleecker Street.' I couldn't believe my ears. Me? Performing off

Broadway? I was over the moon at just the thought of it. Of course I leapt at the chance – I would've flown to New York right that second if I could.

Performing in Manhattan was a huge milestone. You can imagine the narration in my head: 'Wee Janey from Shettleston steps off the subway and takes in the summer heat of New York, as she walks to Bleecker Street theatre to act in her own play. Then she wakes up to discover it's all a dream and she has no shoes to go to school and her life is doomed from there.' Even the voice in my head couldn't take it all in.

I'd visited Manhattan once before, in the late nineties, to hang out with a pal of mine, Shona, and to try out some open spots there. It was the first time I'd carried my own passport and money as an adult, which was a whole new experience. Back then, Sean had a steely grip on the finances and I was like a cheeky child asking for pocket money. How things change.

I fell in love with New York the very first time I saw it. How incredible it was to walk down Fifth Avenue and through Central Park and see all the sights I had grown up with on TV; to walk around Times Square at 2 a.m., drink in coffee shops, eat New York-style pizza. I saw cops chasing cars, I rode the subway, I took buses – the city was full of noise and smells and was everything I hoped it would be.

Unfortunately New York didn't love me quite as much at that point. I managed to get an open spot at Pips comedy club in Sheepshead Bay (not the best-sounding name for a district but in Glasgow we had a maternity hospital called the Rottenrow). There was no audience, just other comics and a New Yorker who told us how to do comedy. It was weird, there were about fifteen people getting up doing five minutes of 'Woody Allen' or *Seinfeld* material. Compared with the melodic American accents, my Glasgow one sounded like metal bin lids being thrown down an escalator. No one could understand me – until I called them 'funny cunts'. They understood that (and laughed for the first time).

Coming back for the second time was just so exciting. This time, I stayed in a friend of a friend's flat right slap-bang in the middle of Manhattan, which was handy, with the ever-supportive John Fleming. John worked alongside Cal Wynter, and he had been looking after my career in a sense ever since he helped me land my first book deal. He gave great advice, he loved my play, and he was fun to be around, so it was great to have him with me.

I was completely blown away by the Americans' reaction to the play. I didn't see any reviews in the press – Bleecker Street was a pretty small theatre – but the response from the crowd after each performance was incredible. So many people came to see it – there was a full house most nights – and I even got a standing ovation. I was overjoyed. Although I'm sure the Americans couldn't completely understand my East End accent, they seemed to get the gist of it. After all, the heroin epidemic wasn't just a Scottish problem.

It was a roasting hot summer in Manhattan, so, poor John, I dragged him down to Brighton Beach in Brooklyn in a heatwave and we ate hot dogs on the sand and played all the weird and wacky games on the pier. Luckily, he is still a good pal to this day – one of my loudest cheerleaders.

Now that things were better in my marriage, and Sean's mental health was on the up, he was willing and able to travel with me. I was booked to perform at a small festival in Toronto, and he jumped at the chance to come with me. He wasn't usually keen on travelling, and we hadn't been abroad as a couple in an age, but for whatever reason he had always wanted to go to Canada. We were super excited about seeing Toronto together. Plus, we could now afford to rent a decent serviced apartment instead of both of us being cooped up in a pokey hotel room.

I was booked to perform in Toronto as part of a newly formed festival, but even before we left Scotland the booker was being bizarrely evasive. He wasn't giving us full information about what we were doing or where we were staying. This wasn't normal, but it didn't put us off – a job is a job after all. Then we landed in Toronto airport, to find no one was waiting for us. We were left stranded in arrivals, and this was before iPhones or WhatsApp, so it was a good old phone box to the rescue until we could buy a Canadian burner phone to use during the stay. I called the promoter's office, but there was no answer.

This wasn't a good start. With my tendency to get fractious in airports and Sean slowly spiralling into an autistic meltdown as our plans went awry, he had to walk out of the airport and round the block to calm down. The promoter was nowhere to be seen. I sat and waited, not so patiently, while gritting my teeth.

Eventually we caught up with him. Normally I would have snapped his face off, but it was immediately obvious to see that he was abjectly sorry and had just bitten off far more than he could ever chew with putting this event together. So I just felt sorry for him. Sean got himself a phone and, once we finally got to the apartment, we both set about trying to help him organise the shows.

Sean proved his weight in gold on that trip. Thank God I took him with me, because the whole thing was a shambles – as some small festivals can be – but Sean managed to keep me on track, bolster me up and make me laugh. The ticket sales were terrible, but we had a good time regardless. And it worked out alright in the end – at one of the gigs, which was a tight twenty-minute set with a tiny audience and hardly any laughs, it turned out someone in the small crowd was pretty important.

In the break, as I walked through the foyer of the theatre, I met Mark Breslin, the owner of the Canadian comedy chain Yuk Yuk's, and he let me know how impressed he was by my work. That wee festival had been pretty much a wipeout, but it resulted in me touring Canada a few more times with a huge comedy chain in the years to come.

So sometimes the things that go wrong can end up right. That story had a happy ending, but sometimes things just go wrong and there's nothing you can do about it.

Throughout the noughties, my wee stepmum Mamie had been living with cancer. It's fair to say your sixties are the sniper years, like some medical assassin has you in their sights and is coming to get you when you least expect it. As I was to find out for myself.

Mamie dealt with chemotherapy, cancer, wigs and a colostomy bag with utter grace and quiet determination. Looking back, I don't know if I appreciated how hard her life was, but now with my own experience of cancer and chemo I wish I could have done more for her. Mamie had her own family as well as us to lean on, which was good, but it was a real tough time.

Despite coping with recurring cancer and all its complications, she and my dad continued to go on their yearly cruises, and enjoy life to the full. At one point, after years of dealing with such a horrific illness, Mamie even seemed to be truly on the mend – I thought her cancer was gone. I thought she was going to be fine.

But in reality, the cancer had been back for some time, and I was completely unaware. She didn't tell anybody until she slowly started to fade away again. Now, having cancer myself, I know how important it is to have those conversations with loved ones. But that was typical Mamie – a stoic woman who never wanted to cause a fuss. By the time I learned the truth, Mamie only had a few months left to live.

When Mamie died, Dad was bereft. They had almost made it to their twenty-fifth wedding anniversary, second time round for both of them. She was such a force for good in our lives, she was always so kind, her dinners were legendary, her driving was brilliant and she just loved people. She was an amazing woman, and I was so lucky to have her as stepmum. I still miss her dearly.

It was clear Dad would need some looking after now he was on his own, and it was our job as a family to

111

provide that care. My sister Ann and brother David were a brilliant help, as tough as things were in their own day-to-day lives. Ann had her husband, Brian, to look after, who had severely deteriorated with MS, though she did her best with visits and phone calls; David was recovering from an industrial accident that left him immobile. But the three of us did everything we could to be there for Dad.

At the same time my eldest brother Jim – who had been dealing with his own issues for years – was needing care of his own, too.

Jim had struggled with heroin addiction for many years, and had contracted HIV as a result. This had spurred me to try to raise awareness about HIV back when people didn't want to discuss it.

HIV and AIDS destroy your body's immune system, leaving you vulnerable to all sorts of awful diseases. It broke my heart to find out that, around the time Mamie was seriously ill with cancer in the late noughties, Jim developed non-Hodgkin lymphoma. Now he was going through chemo.

My whole family had a complicated relationship with Jim. He and I were very close as adults, but it was hard making peace with how he had behaved in my childhood. Jim and my mum fought like cat and dog after Dad left in the seventies, and he was a physical bully to us younger kids, but he was always mentally unstable and given to depression. I tried my best to help him, but Jim took a lot of time and energy to cope with. Although, when I got married and had the pub, we became much closer.

Jim lived in Bo'ness, which is between Glasgow and Edinburgh on the banks of the Firth of Forth. When Mamie was ill, I would get the bus or train through to see him twice a month and stay with him for the day. Every time I visited his wee flat it would be total chaos. Jim could collect junk and dirt like nobody I'd ever met before.

In his living room, there were three televisions stacked on top of one another – one with volume, one with the picture, and one for good luck. There was a broken guitar and, at one point, a three-legged cat. He also had a huge collection of knives and swords, and an array of fake guns and fake weapons to boot. If a fake war ever broke out, Jim would be the man to win the conflict.

As if Jim's house wasn't chaotic enough, he also had a big galumphing mongrel called Cooper who would charge through the clutter to try to have sex with your legs on meeting. Jim would shout, 'Don't do that Cooper, that's your auntie!' as if the incest part was worse than a dog shagging your legs.

Cooper had a fabulous fascination with the bright plastic clothes pegs that were stuck to the washing line, out in Jim's communal garden. He would leap up to extraordinary heights to snap the pegs off the line. Unfortunately, Jim's chemotherapy port was a red plastic clip on his body and, when he showed me this, Cooper tried to bite it off his chest.

Jim liked to smoke weed and his coffee table was always covered in cannabis grinds. Cooper would swish his big tail, clear the table and sweep the lot into the one-bar electric fire. The smell of burnt weed would knock you out.

It was bedlam – dog barking, Jim shouting, and me trying to heat up a dinner in the manky kitchen. I would clean the flat and buy him food when I visited, and the next week it would revert to a sink full of dirty dishes and a toilet bowl that looked like someone had packed earth down it to grow leeks. Those who know me know that I have serious emotional issues with dirty houses, because of the squalor I lived in for most of my childhood. But I loved Jim, so I did my best to help him have some semblance of a clean and tidy place to live, especially with the chemo and his low immunity.

Eventually, Jim moved down to Colchester to be near his daughter. I knew he was growing weaker, and, many phone calls later, it felt like he was not coping well. But I underestimated how bad he was, and Jim hadn't been good at letting me know.

Then, on New Year's Eve 2010, I spotted a post on Facebook from Jim's granddaughter that read, 'Gone but not forgotten Granda Jim'. That's how I found out my brother had died. On fucking Facebook.

My dad was devastated at the news, so soon after Mamie. I'd kept him informed of Jim's progress because their relationship had been strained through many years of Jim asking him for money to go to rehab but then letting him down by spending it on drugs instead. Still, Dad never gave up on him and, no matter how bad things were, would always give me cash to help Jim with his shopping. But there came a time when Jim began to respectfully keep his distance, knowing he was only hurting Dad and Mamie with his drug use and chaotic lifestyle.

My dad had struggled with an alcohol addiction of his own. But by this point he'd been sober for nearly thirty years and his regular sobriety meetings were now a lifeline for him. They gave him a sense of community and fellowship that he had never experienced while he was drinking. He once told me how isolating the drink was for him. I remember the difference it made to him when he joined Alcoholics Anonymous, and the lifelong pals he made. So many times after he got sober he told me how sorry he was for not being around enough when I was wee. AA was his saving grace.

Dad was lucky to have so many friends and family around him, but no one could fill the hole that Mamie left.

Sean and I did our best to keep Dad company. We even ripped out his entire back garden and made it a lot easier to look after. He loved sitting out there in the sunshine with all the open space and decking, which worked so much better for his mobility, too. We had to keep him under constant watch, though – it was becoming clear that his own health was slowly but steadily declining. So, Sean was up at his house daily to make sure he was fed and had taken his meds.

Once, when Ashley and I were in Los Angeles doing some gigs, I called Dad to check in on him, but when he answered I could only hear mumbling; he wasn't making sense. My stomach lurched. I immediately knew he was having a stroke. When I hung up on him to call Sean, completely frantic, I was painfully aware that it could have been the last time I would hear my dad's voice. Sean dropped everything, drove up to Dad's and got him into hospital.

Sean sat all night with him and wouldn't leave his side until the doctors had seen him. He didn't want Dad to be there alone and confused. I can never thank Sean enough for that kindness because, thankfully, although Dad did recover from the many little strokes he had that day, it was clear that he was going to need more help from now on. Worse still, it wasn't long before dementia started to take hold as well.

Dad and Sean hadn't always got on. It wasn't my dad's fault, Sean just didn't really befriend anyone on my side, or his own to be honest, though he was very fond of Mamie. He was always just respectful and polite to my dad, but now with Dad's dementia diagnosis it was Sean who really stepped up to look after him. While I was away working, he would take Dad out in the car and on visits to little villages and coffee shops across Scotland. He started going to Dad's house every day, arranging his medicine, his GP appointments, making sure his dinners were there and his fridge was full. Dad now had a carer coming in daily and a social worker to help with all his needs, too. Soon I was having to share his bank account to pay his bills as he became more confused and anxious about his money.

He'd been such a good daddy that it was always easy to be around him and show our respect and love. Plus, he was funny as fuck. He'd always loved to tease us. When my siblings and I were small, he used to draw cartoons of us sitting on a potty doing the toilet, which he would then threaten to show to all our friends at school. Or he would often pretend that he had a dead mouse and chase us around the house with a bit of grey wool. He would terrify us with horrific ghost stories, too – to this day white Scottie dogs creep me out, all because Dad told me that once a black one had run down our close stairs and seen a ghost and turned white. For years I thought all white Scottie dogs had been traumatised by a nearby ghost.

Now, in his final years, he was just the same. Sometimes when I came round to the house to look after him, he would pretend to be dead when I came through the door – he would lie on the floor at the bottom of the stairs and get up laughing when I screamed. It nearly gave me a stroke every time. He was a proper joker.

Even as he grew frailer, he never lost his sense of humour. We would spend afternoons watching telly in his house, making up voices for the people we saw on screen. Just like Ashley and I still do – that's where the voice-overs originated. Or we would sit out in his lovely garden as he used a laser pen to entertain the cat next door, or he would wage a war on the squirrels who kept eating the bird food.

We used to do exercises together for his weak arms – I would come at him with a cushion and say 'I'm going to kill you!' (joking, obviously) and he would push the cushion back at me. We would scream with laughter at our darkly comic game. It would later end in an awkward enquiry when we were caught doing it in front of his carer, who had come in to check on him. Thankfully,

Dad was mentally competent enough to assure the carers I wasn't actually trying to kill him. Although every now and then he'd say, 'Don't leave me alone with her.'

Dad had stairs in his house, which was a cause for concern as he had become prone to stumbling. So when he began to struggle more, physically, we helped as much as we could – Sean organised for his bath to be removed and replaced with a walk-in shower, and grip rails to be installed.

Every Friday night when I was home, Sean and I would have a fish supper dinner with Dad. He would set the table and make a big pot of tea, ready for us to arrive with an enormous bag of salty, vinegary fish and chips wrapped in brown paper. We all loved those nights, sitting together, eating and laughing and drinking gallons of tea. Of course it was hard watching my dad grow weaker, but I treasured the time I got to spend with him.

Eventually, we had no choice but to move him to a care home. It was the hardest decision I have ever made. I couldn't have him stay with me as I didn't have a spare bedroom in the flat. Thankfully, the home was the block next to ours, which meant that Sean, Ashley and I could see him three to four times a day if we wanted.

I remember crying my eyes out one night as he sat and held my hand. 'Janey, you did the best thing,' he whispered as I explained how I felt like I was letting him

119

down by putting him there. My dad had always supported me, now I felt that I was abandoning him. The guilt was overwhelming. And seeing him alone in the care home was heartbreaking. So we surrounded his bed with photos of him and all the family; both he and Mamie had had such a full life, with so many friends, and many of them came to visit him in the care home. Proper old Glasgow pals – that sense of family and community came through when he needed it most. It was nice for me to see some old relatives who I hadn't seen in years come over to sit with Dad.

Aside from chatting with his daily visitors, Dad wasn't really into the social side of the home. He preferred to sit in his room and listen to the radio. Luckily, it was around this time Ashley got her own show on BBC Radio Scotland on a Friday night. Dad and I would tune in and he would laugh at her jokes and chatter. He was so proud of her.

When Dad's death finally came in 2017 it was in the middle of the night. I was at home when the landline rang with the news from the nursing home. I always knew when the landline rang it would be news about my dad. When he died, I disconnected the phone, because I knew there was no one else that called that number.

Dad's death devastated us all, especially Ashley. The two of them had always been incredibly close; he attended every school play, concert and Christmas-carol performance in Glasgow's Princes Square. He and Mamie were absolutely the best grandparents anyone could ask for. They made every Halloween fabulous for Ashley and all the wee kids in their cul-de-sac; they spoiled her rotten like grannies and grandads are meant to. We were blessed with them both.

I felt so lucky, too, that Dad told me I was loved almost every single day of my life. He never once made me feel I had let him down, though I am sure I did a few times. He always embraced my creativity. He even taught me how to paint and draw; it was one of his hobbies. When I was emptying his house, I found expensive paintbrushes and, on the back of the packet, there was a little note that said 'For Janey from Pop'. His once-beautiful handwriting was so shaky, almost indecipherable. He knew he couldn't paint again and had put them aside for me. I wept buckets when I found those brushes. I still miss him every day.

12

THROUGH EVERY SINGLE hardship I've faced in my adult life, it's been the women in my circle who have truly stood by me. Whenever I felt at odds with the world, whenever I wasn't being listened to, whenever I was struggling in any way, it has always been women who got me through, stuck beside me, and lifted me up. Women like my inimitable girlfriends Monica and Elaine and my rock, Shirley.

Shirley had, and still has, so many amazing qualities. She's an organisational pro, and she's a dab hand at filling in forms. She'll go the extra mile to help me when I need it – when my dad passed away, Shirley organised the whole funeral. But before that, back in 2012, with her help I decided to apply to the Scottish Arts Council for funding to go to the Women in Comedy Festival in Boston.

By this stage in my career I'd performed at loads of

comedy festivals, but this one was different. I'd never been to an all-female festival before. Usually, women were outnumbered by men at those sorts of spaces – the men would dominate, and the women got a sliver of the attention. So I was desperate to head to Boston to check out this comedy anomaly.

The thing about arts councils is that the people who can fill in all the forms with such expertise aren't always great at putting on shows and the people who are really good at comedy can't fill in forms. To be fair, the arts council in question – ironically – didn't support comedy back then – I don't know if they do now – so I had to call it 'storytelling', even though the festival was called 'Women in Comedy'.

Shirley helped me to create a Fringe workshop to explain how to bring a show to the Edinburgh Fringe to a forum of American female comics. She wrote screeds of paragraphs explaining the outcomes, the format, the reasons for going, the budget – you name it, she covered it.

Lo and behold we were granted some cash and we were off to Boston. I used my British Airways Airmiles companion flight for Shirley and she organised our stay in a stunning nineteenth-century brownstone full of original fittings and antiques. Our room had big single beds with brown wooden headboards, a proper old-fashioned bathtub and a wee kitchen. It was like a museum, right on Commonwealth Avenue in the city centre. I kept expecting to meet an ancient ghostly president on the grand staircase, where a creepy mannequin dressed as a British Redcoat stood halfway up the stairs.

Shirley and I had a fabulous time in Boston – we always had fun together. Though when we had first met, a couple of years earlier, it was in much less cheery circumstances.

I'd got talking to Simon Pegg in the Groucho and he had told me he had a Glasgow auntie. He said we should get together, because she's a firebrand and a gab, just like me. I resisted – I had enough pals, I thought – but he gave me her mobile number, just in case I changed my mind.

Not long after that when I was in London again, I heard the terrible news that Jason Wood, a comedy pal of mine, had passed away suddenly. I was in shock and completely devastated; it was a tremendous loss for so many of us in the comedy community. Jason was so well loved, such a brilliant singer and comedian, and his sudden death at such a young age just really affected me.

For no reason I can explain, I called Shirley – a complete stranger – who also happened to be in London, and blurted out that a friend had died and I needed to talk. It wasn't really the way to start a new friendship but Shirley was so practical and empathetic on the phone, so we decided to meet up when we were both back in Glasgow. I always believe Jason sent me Shirley that day – like a gift, she was given to me. She's been my rock ever since.

Now here we were in Boston and Shirley and I were loving it. My gig was in a pub across from the famous gated Harvard University. We had expected bespectacled academics walking about with books in hand and small pubs with people reciting poetry or groups of young people sitting on the grass studying in silence. Instead it was quite the eye-opener as we saw so many homeless people pushing old creaky shopping carts full of clothes and plastic bottles. I'd obviously watched too many episodes of *Gilmore Girls*.

The gig itself was a huge success, and it was a breath of fresh air to be surrounded by so many talented and creative women all in one place. Although Shirley wouldn't have been able to say how well my performance went, as she sat on the stairs of the venue playing Angry Birds the whole time. In fairness to her, she'd seen me gig loads by then. That's Shirley for you, and to this day she still sits at the side of the stage and plays games on her phone. I think she's probably bored to death by comedy, having me as a best friend and Simon Pegg as a nephew.

But our time in Boston was definitely worth all the hideous paperwork. We have such great synergy, and love to explore new places together. We walked the streets of the city for hours, admiring the beautiful brownstone buildings that reminded us of the fancier tenements back in Glasgow. Just as we said that, we turned down a street that led to one of the dodgier parts of town, where a humongous slavering beast of a dog went for both of us and we had to run full pelt all the way down Commonwealth Avenue. It really was like being back in Glasgow.

One of the best moments of my life was soon to follow. When I talk about the incredible women who surround me, of course that includes my daughter Ashley, and I feel so fortunate that she was there to witness it, in one of my favourite places – New Zealand.

We'd made the trip over for a tour, and what a tour it turned out to be. Ashley immediately slipped into manager mode and looked after me. She took videos of everything, making a sort of unofficial documentary of all the gigs I was doing and all the places we went. It brought me so much joy for the two of us to share that.

We had a fabulous time in Auckland before leaving for Wellington. We got on that strange flight where the plane basically drops out of the sky on the really wee Wellington runway. I remember Ashley had too much luggage, so one of the tour managers took some of her belongings in his bag. Going through security, a big phallic thing showed up in his bag on the X-ray and when they took his bag aside and questioned him he was dumbfounded as to what it was. It was only Ashley's podcast microphone that he was carrying for us, but Ashley and I did say 'huge dildo' in unison to the security man.

We couldn't wait to check in at the awesome Museum Hotel, which is utterly gorgeous and full of stunning art pieces. But we were also anxious to get there for another reason – there was gossip that Billy Connolly was staying at the same hotel.

Ashley and I were beside ourselves at the thought of being in the same place as the Big Yin. What if we met him? What if we sat beside each other at breakfast? What if we became pals? I was beyond excited.

But something happened that made me cringe. Every day, the hotel would slip a note about the weather and about comedy shows at the festival under every door. So they slipped under Billy's door a note that read, 'Come see Janey Godley at the International Comedy festival and see why the press call her the female Billy Connolly!' Yes, it was true, the press did call me the female Billy Connolly. Still it was pretty mortifying. I was horrified to think of him reading it and being furious, or calling me out and saying he'd heard I was shit or something worse . . . It just made me feel very uncomfortable.

I certainly had to stem the overwhelming desire to stalk every corridor and break into his room to remove that stupid note, but I thought better of it and eventually came up with the idea instead to leave a copy of my autobiography *Handstands in the Dark* at reception for him with a short note. Just thinking that he might read my book was enough for me.

That afternoon, Ashley and I were sitting having a cup of tea in the most beautiful hotel room we have ever been in when the room phone rang.

'Hello, Billy Connolly here,' the familiar Glaswegian voice boomed out.

'Get fucked you cunts, who is this? Is that you, Terry Alderton?' I really believed it was Terry, an amazing British comic who was at the comedy festival with us. Terry is really good at voices, and all the other comics had heard about me giving Billy my book.

'Nope, it's me, Billy. You want to meet in the lobby for a cup of tea?' he suggested. It took a moment for it to sink in that it was him.

I squeaked a yes, and put the phone down.

The thought of being face-to-face with my hero sent me into a frenzy. I ran about my hotel room pulling off my pyjamas and pulling a bra on outside in as Ashley looked on in bewilderment. I ran a brush through my mental hair, grabbed my bag and went racing down to the lifts.

'Mum for fuck's sake calm down, you look like Kathy Bates in *Misery*, he will be terrified you are going to hobble him!' Ashley said. And 'Breathe, and calm down!' she urged as I frantically pressed all the lift buttons but the one for the ground floor.

Eventually, after what felt like forty-five minutes, the lift reached the ground floor. I spotted myself in the mirror and I indeed looked like a woman who had escaped from a hostage situation. I breathed slowly and walked calmly into the foyer. Billy Connolly came towards me, dressed sharp and looking good, and hugged me close. 'Let's get tea,' he said.

After introductions, Ashley got us a tea tray, said hello and then excused herself by explaining that she was going to see *The Avengers* and said her goodbyes.

Billy and I chatted for over an hour. I managed to calm down, and tried hard not to gabble and talk utter shite. He has a way of putting you at ease – he is such a warm, genuinely lovely man. Plus, he is really attractive.

I met my hero and I totally fell in love with him.

We laughed, we talked comedy, we talked art, we

talked books, we talked Glasgow, and then he said, 'I'll come see your show tonight.'

'Please don't, it would be like singing karaoke in front of Elvis,' I replied. He laughed. 'I'm a great audience member – I laugh and I love comedy.'

I didn't believe he would come – not that I thought he was a liar, I just thought he was being polite. But still, Ashley and I headed up to the San Fran Bath House venue in Cuba Street and explained to the ticket man that Billy Connolly might turn up. The man nodded and rolled his eyes. It felt like we were fantasists who regularly claimed famous people were our pals.

However, the venue manager, Ziggy, was over the moon, and the staff were delighted about the prospect of our lovely venue hosting such a star. I felt bad; if he didn't turn up, the prospect of sharing the room with me for an hour would disappoint them.

I was giddy when Billy came to the door early and Ashley met him and walked him up. The venue was closed to the public as they got the room ready, but the staff were cool as hell – although definitely overwhelmed – and made the big man and me a cup of tea as he settled down near the back with Ashley.

The look on my punters' faces as they rocked up to the bar to buy drinks and turned round to see Billy Connolly just tickled me pink.

Ashley and Billy sat down to share a pizza as the show started. I was hyper aware, as I walked out onto that stage, that everyone in the room knew Billy Connolly was sitting there watching me. My long-time comedy hero, sitting beside my daughter with hands clasped, staring at the stage. My heart skipped a beat, the lights blinded me. Then I said, 'Hello Wellington, how are you?' and the cheers started.

The show went really well. I did my stuff – I riffed, I chatted to the crowd, I made good laughs and claps and I forgot he was there. I forgot Billy Connolly was sitting watching. Until I heard his big hearty laugh and then my heart boomed again and the show went on. There were some odd heckles, which I embraced and which actually made the show even better, and soon the lights dimmed and I was standing in front of my idol again.

He put his two big arms round me, hugged me close and said, 'That was brilliant, you are so unafraid up there.' My heart swelled with pride as he continued, 'You know the craft so well. There is no such thing as female or male comedy, there is just comedy, and *you* are comedy Janey. The way you calmly held them in your hand and took them on a journey – everything was just amazing, well done!'

It was the best endorsement ever. Can you imagine the King of Comedy telling you he liked your work? I almost peed myself with excitement.

I know even if I'd died onstage, he would have said nice things, but it was a good show – as a seasoned one-woman show performer of over ten years I know the difference, and it was a good 'un – thank GOD!

Billy and I went onto the balcony. He lit a cigar before quoting all the bits he loved and replaying how they made him laugh. I forgot he was a huge star and he, Ashley and I nattered at each other for ages, and then walked back to our hotel together.

Here's the thing: I thought Billy Connolly watching me do comedy was scary. No, walking through the busy roads of Wellington with Billy Connolly was terrifying – he doesn't give a fuck about the green man, he just marches onto busy roads. Ashley felt compelled to walk beside him and I ran like a wee hobbit behind them, visualising my daughter being battered by a car alongside Billy Connolly! He and Ashley were like big Highlanders tramping through the glens of heather, no sideways glances, just big Scottish arms swinging, carefree. Weirdly, cars stopped, as if in homage to their presence.

It was the most amazing night. I always knew one day I would meet him but I did *not* know it would end with me almost getting knocked down by a car behind him at the other end of the world.

When we got back into our hotel room, I looked at Ashley and burst into tears. That was, without a doubt, one of the best moments of my life and I couldn't verbalise how it made me feel. Crying was easier.

Getting back to the UK and working the circuit doing Jongleurs, the Stand and the regular clubs was fine and dandy for me now. I wasn't scared any more; the thing back in 1995 that terrified me was long gone. Having Billy endorse me was such a huge confidence boost – it didn't matter what was being said about me online or in cliquey comedy clubs, Billy Connolly liked my comedy show, so I would be floating on a cloud of happiness for the foreseeable future.

13

I WAS PROUD of myself – I had managed to keep my family financially afloat, we were stable, and we were happy. Ashley graduated from university with a degree in film-making and was doing comedy, sketch shows, acting and writing for radio; Sean was getting psychological help and support for his autism. Things were ticking along just fine. Plus, I had a new agent, Chris Davis. We had been introduced by my agent at the time, Michael Vine, in the Groucho. Michael is over-the-top fabulous, and doesn't beat around the bush; he introduced me to Chris and said, 'He's very suited to you – he'll be a better agent than me!' So, Chris and I had a meeting, completely hit it off, and have been practically inseparable ever since.

With Chris's expertise, and thanks to a pretty good social media presence, my fan base continued to grow. I was using Facebook to show off my comedy videos, and

Twitter to connect with new fans from live shows. Of course, I also used Twitter to argue with strangers, but we'll get to that.

I was delighted that, despite once having been adamant that stand-up wasn't her thing, Ashley was now back at it. I had been itching for us to perform together for years, and the opportunity came our way when it was announced that the Commonwealth Games were coming to Glasgow. It was a big deal for the city. To celebrate, Ashley and I – with the help of Claire McCauley – created a programme called 'Journeys to Glasgow', where we travelled around Scotland to small venues and libraries, gathering stories from locals about their trips to Glasgow. Of course, we did some stand-up along the way. Ashley was gaining so much confidence and it was brilliant to travel on the road as a team and watch her onstage.

In one of the libraries where Ashley and I had set up a space to record stories from the public, a quite ordinary-looking man waited his turn in the queue and sat down beside us. He was very mild-mannered and softly spoken. He told us he was a big fan of our comedy, and went on to tell us the tale of how he met his beloved wife and brought her back to Glasgow, where they raised a family. What a sweet story, we thought. Unfortunately we had to cut him from the programme post-production, as it transpired he had gone on to kill his wife and was serving time in jail. Not the kind of message we wanted on our Commonwealth project.

Travelling round far-flung villages and towns in Scotland, talking about journeys in small libraries and wee town halls, was just brilliant fun. The Commonwealth year was a fabulous time to showcase our city. I recall it being the hottest summer in ages, and even the hard-bitten Glaswegians managed to kick back and enjoy the crowds and street cafes in the sunshine.

I'd also now started running a comedy club in the Candleriggs, down in the Merchant City, at a beautiful new venue called Wild Cabaret. The owner, Tony Kelly, saw me doing stand-up and, against all my protests, managed to talk me into running a Thursday-night comedy gig – I was reluctant to run a gig again, as I hate paperwork and dealing with people, but it was a huge success and would run for about six years. My time spent there taught me so much about comedy and giving new comics a chance to have their own voices heard. There was an open mic slot where comics could turn up on the night and try out, whether it was their first ever gig or their thirtieth. I knew how some comedy promoters would gatekeep their clubs, making new acts jump through hoops or be part of a clique before they could get access to the stage. I made sure I was the opposite; anyone could turn up and do five or ten minutes and I would fit them in. It was hit and miss, and making sure audiences get the right comics at the right time in the show is hard work and takes a lot of practice. But I loved the whole experience, and Tony and I are best pals to this day.

In the background during this time was the Scottish independence campaign. I was fully on the side of independence. I truly believe Scotland can make its own decisions and not be governed by Westminster. Of course, declaring this publicly started a huge pushback on social media from those who disagreed with my standpoint. If only I'd known how getting involved in politics would come back to bite me further down the line. But the fight was in me and I couldn't stop myself from heading in.

I had helped campaign and I openly spoke out against the union, and that became a toxic subject on social media. In the west of Scotland in particular, the independence debate raised the issue of sectarianism – Catholics and Protestants started to draw up battle lines, with football clubs being dragged into the fray. It's so confusing for people on the outside to understand why football and religion in Scotland become embroiled in party politics. Scottish Tories and union-ists are often and sometimes mistakenly associated with Rangers football club, allegiance with the royal family, and Protestantism; Scottish independence supporters are assumed to be anti-royal, Catholic, Celtic fans. These stereotypes tend to be magnified on Twitter and Facebook and don't really reflect the actual population.

I was called a Catholic (I'm not), I was called a Celtic football fan (I'm not). I am a Protestant, Rangers football fan who supports independence. In Glasgow.

When I found myself getting into Twitter fights with people after I nailed my colours to the mast and showed support for independence, I almost enjoyed it, in a strange way. I liked proving people wrong, and I was well used to countering ridiculous arguments about football and religion, given that I worked in a pub in the East End for fifteen years – that was my forte. I didn't fully understand the power of social media then. I was naïve. I just thought everyone could argue and say what they wanted but it would be done with when you logged off. It started to affect me, though, when I was getting death and rape threats.

It only got worse when Scotland lost the referendum. The more passionate Scottish unionists paraded in George Square, many causing trouble by throwing flares and climbing over the public statues. Some right-wing extremists bedecked in union flags were shown to be throwing 'Hitler salutes' in newspaper images.

Losing the referendum was very disappointing for many of us and online it became the battleground for all the anger from both sides. It didn't help that I continued to argue back. Many Scottish comics were pro-Indy and so there was a general online seething towards comedians. But I was one of the main targets as I was one of the most vocal.

Some far-right football groups would put links to my tweets on their own chatrooms to encourage pile-ons of abuse. It was distressing, to say the least. But despite having to get the police involved a few times when the abuse became credible threats, still I argued back – I wasn't going to be silenced. I was worried about walking to local gigs as I had been told online that the men who argued with me had been watching my gig list and promised to attack me on my way to shows. Thankfully it never happened; they kept all their threats to anonymous online hate.

There were hundreds of instances over the years of strangers sending me abusive, hateful tweets. Even some MPs trolled me and sent me abuse online. One particular man stalked me online and sent daily abuse claiming my husband was in the IRA, that we were drug dealers, and even suggested I had lied about the past child abuse. I had to twice get lawyers and police on to him.

In the months and years after the independence referendum, and as the 2016 Brexit referendum approached, social media in Scotland grew full of people defending President Trump and supporting right-wing causes. As if that wasn't bad enough, it was amidst all the Brexit referendum chaos that I heard Trump was coming to Scotland, to his golf resort in Turnberry on the west coast. So I decided to give him a true Glasgow welcome.

Donald and I had history; back in 2012 he had tweeted that another one of his Scottish golf courses, in Aberdeen, had been ravaged by a storm. So I tweeted back (not expecting a reply), 'Haha Your golf course has fallen into the sea'.

'no, it held up to storm very well', came his response. I was stunned he had time to reply to an ordinary wee Glasgow woman like me.

'maybe you can side comb the grass over the hole', I replied. That's when he blocked me.

Trump's visit to Turnberry fell on the day of the Brexit result. I didn't care what anyone said, the Leave campaign was built on basic racism against immigrants and asylum-seekers.

Trump had been accused of racism throughout his career, going back to when he called for the death penalty for young innocent black teens for a rape in Central Park back in 1989. I despised everything he stood for; he was a bully, and he treated women like meat, too. So, on that day in June, I got a piece of lino and reversed it, took a blue sharpie pen and wrote 'Trump is a cunt' boldly on the white side.

I rolled it up, packed a bag and headed into George Square, where a bus was waiting to take protesters down to Turnberry.

As we pulled in to the wee bus stop at Turnberry, we could see the big white hotel on the rise of the hill in front of us, with the Trump helicopter parked outside the front door. There was a heavy police presence and the cops immediately told us we could protest but we had to stay kettled in the bus stop area.

I decided I wasn't doing that; I gave a pal my phone and said, 'I'm going to stand over there in front of his hotel and unfurl my poster, make sure you get the helicopter and the hotel in the photo.' There were no kids or passers-by around, so it felt safe enough to have the sweary word on show.

The minute I opened the banner, my pal snapped a few pictures as the cops came over to tell me I wasn't to use that word in public. I did explain I could put my

142

hand over the letter 'C' so it would read 'UNT' and they had a wee debate about that but decided it wasn't to be.

They told me I had to go back to the bus stop. I explained I wouldn't be doing that as the Scottish pavements didn't belong to Mr Trump and I was free to walk up and down them. I promised not to unfurl my bad-word banner and I sat at the gates of Trump Turnberry instead. They tried everything to move me but I stayed put.

Two well-dressed American men in full suits and overcoats in the Scottish heat came down and told me they would have me arrested. I just stared at them and said, 'Mate, you can't arrest me, I am a Scottish citizen on Scottish land and I am not sure you even have a visa big enough to arrest me. If we were in America, you could probably shoot me, but not here my friend.'

The local police laughed, and I laughed even louder as the angry men in overcoats stormed back up the steps.

Many of the cops that day agreed with my thoughts about Trump and let me carry on my protest. The ones who spoke to me agreed he was nothing but a twat and fully endorsed my poster. One or two cops told me that as long as I kept it hidden they would support me protesting.

There were news teams and press wandering about the entrance to the hotel and I spotted a furore at one of the windows. I suspected Mr Trump was raging that I couldn't be moved.

After what turned out to be a pretty fun day giving Donald a piece of our mind, us protesters headed back on the bus for George Square. I uploaded the image of me holding my poster with Trump's flashy helicopter behind me to Twitter and Facebook, not expecting much of a reaction.

By 5 p.m. that night, the photo had gone viral and the press were on the phone.

So many people loved the image but, as is always the case with social media, for almost every positive reaction there was a negative one too. The threats and abuse piled in, and of course I argued back on Twitter like I always did. Many Scottish unionists and Rangers football fans were absolutely raging at my protest and demanded that I be cancelled for using such bad language and for being rude.

I quickly realised that the people who hated me for calling out Trump were mostly men and mostly right-wing. They created fake racist and anti-Semitic tweets to try to get me cancelled. Even Channel 4's most famous cat impersonator George Galloway had to apologise for retweeting them. It was a full-on onslaught online, all because I slagged off Trump.

I stood my ground and my protest became my next comedy show, called *Donald Trump is a Cunt*. I went on the road and sold out up and down the UK. Meanwhile, the online abuse that was hurled my way escalated beyond belief. I had one persistent troll, let's call him 'Alan', whose tweets were so constant and so vile that we had to get lawyers and cops involved. The abuse went on over years, with him targeting me and other women in the independence camp. Then, out of the blue, he vanished offline. Last I heard he was under arrest for sexually attacking women in Edinburgh. Who knows who hides behind the screen? Well, the joke's on 'Alan' – to this day my 'Trump' cards sell through my website.

The Trump supporters in America piled on the online abuse too. Although they were really rubbish at insults – that was funny. They'd write, 'your mom sucks!' and I'd say, 'my maw's deed and you're a cunt'.

You might think that after all the abuse that came my way I would learn to shut up. I didn't!

I even went back and welcomed Trump on his next visit to Scotland in 2018. This time I made a poster with the words 'Trump is a runt' as I knew I could carefully put my hand over the bottom of the small 'r' and it would look like a 'c'. It worked perfectly and managed to make everyone annoyed, as they couldn't be angry at a misplaced hand. The local cops were expecting me and even high-fived me as I walked past with the poster. This absolutely delighted many of my fans online. Yet again it made global news and brought more grief to my door, but, as you know, I liked arguing back.

The upside of all the attention the Trump protest brought was that I gained so many new fans, and I became the 'Trump's a cunt woman'. It resonated with so many people and now so many more wanted to see me live. I got a huge amount of support online, too. Turns out I wasn't alone in my opinion of Trump – and also, with new hindsight, wasn't I right?

14

MY CAREER WAS keeping me busy – I had new fans, thanks to Donald – and my life was only going to get busier, in ways I couldn't have imagined. There were surprises round every corner (and, at this stage, they were still pleasant surprises). A childhood dream realised, an unexpected addition to the family. But first, my most successful Fringe show yet.

The Fringe was an annual event now for me; I wouldn't miss it. Ashley and I had decided to stop paying big venues so much money now and go with the Free Festival instead. It has a basic model where a performer pays £100 to enrol (although you still have to pay the Fringe Society £350 to be featured in the brochure, which I think is outdated and not worth a penny, but hey) and for that you get a venue, a dedicated brochure, a fabulous constantly updated website and in-house staff. The audience pay what they can afford. You're in charge of promoting your show, but thankfully the internet and social media has loosened the stranglehold on visibility at the Fringe, so there's not such a big need to pay huge amounts for PR or get reviewers in, or to generate front covers of magazines.

After the show, I would stand at the door with a bucket and say to the crowd, 'If you can afford it, please donate, if you are skint please take money out of the bucket!' People would queue up to leave some cash, or just talk to me and share a moment. Some people gave me cakes, some people couldn't afford to pay and gave me a badge or a button instead. It was a wonderful feeling, and folk were so generous. It really felt like an honest transaction between audience and performer.

I'd always felt frustrated with the paid venues, most of all because the London comedy promoters would stand right outside and poach potential gig-goers. I would spend so much time and a lot of money getting people to go out and flyer for me – including Sean and Ashley – and they would traipse around the city for four or five hours, encouraging folk to come to my show. Then people would come to the venue with my flyer in hand, planning to see my show, and outside my venue there would be some other comedy promoter – always with a big agency – who would give out free tickets to someone else's show right at the door. So the people who had flyers for my show, who had planned to come and see me and were ready to buy a ticket, just took a free ticket for someone else at the last minute instead. Of course people were going to take the freebies; could you blame them?

So I loved the idea of the Free Festival, and the crowds of people exploring the most expensive city in Scotland during August appreciated a bargain – people on a budget could still afford to see a good show. And there was less risk of audience members being poached at the last minute.

I made more money on the bucket shows than I ever did on the ticketed Fringe shows – so much so that the bank tellers were growing sceptical about where all the cash was coming from.

The queues were round the block for the shows and Ashley and I were having a ball. There was a certain level of freedom too because it was easier for acts to support each other. You could have lesser-known acts introduce you and help get them an audience for their shows as well. I think it's so important to share your stage time with others and lift them up. I had so many comedians from free venues do a few minutes on my show and then flyer the audience going out. It's the way to do it.

With so many successful years in the business, it's clear that comedy was always my calling, but I never gave up on my dream of being an actor. And now it finally came true, thanks to a little film called *Wild Rose*.

I got the part through my agent – the role was a no-nonsense barmaid (how could I fail?). I was sent for a casting and I did the audition, and the writer actually said she'd always had me in mind because she was a fan of my work and knew I used to work in a bar. So I passed the audition, and I was utterly over the moon.

Soon enough I was in London sitting beside Julie Walters doing a table-read. I met her in the toilets beforehand and I couldn't speak – for the first time in my life I was absolutely speechless. I kept having to pinch myself that this was where my life had taken me. Julie was so brilliant, she just gave me a cuddle as though I was an old pal. She has a knack for making you feel that way.

The film is about a Glasgow girl, played by the brilliantly talented Jessie Buckley, who gets out of prison and has her heart set on being a country music star. She sings in 'my' bar, the Glasgow's Grand Ole Opry, an iconic country music venue in Govan.

The entire experience was mind-blowing. I had some good lines and even a fight scene. I never knew all those years of rolling about on a pub carpet fighting with punters would eventually come in handy. When the time came, I got to attend the red-carpet event at the premiere in London, which was one of the proudest nights of my life. Of course, Ashley was right there with me and, when she saw my name come up on the big screen, began to cry. Actually, we both sniffled through that bit. The film went on to do amazingly well – it won a Scottish BAFTA for best feature film, and received loads of nominations across the indie film awards.

All those years ago, standing in that pub in The Calton, yearning to be an actor – finally in a small way I'd made it happen. My heart was huge; it was everything that wee girl in Shettleston ever dreamed of. Although it was hardly a stretch playing a Glaswegian barmaid!

Life was good, but there was something missing. I had always wanted a dog – I had grown up with pets – but Sean was adamant that we didn't have the lifestyle for one. Who would walk this dog? Who would feed this dog? Not him. His dad had dogs when he was growing up, but they were vicious guard dogs who tried to bite everyone they saw.

One day, Ashley explained that a friend of hers knew a woman who had a wee sausage dog and she was giving it away. She asked if she could just go and see the animal, thinking that maybe if she had a few visits she might bond with it and finally think about adopting it. Sean and I didn't really pay much attention to this conversation.

That night, when I came home after filming a TV show called *The Comedians at the King's*, I walked into my living room to find a tiny, angry dog sitting on my sofa barking at me. Yes, Ashley had intended on just visiting this dog, but its owner had other ideas. The woman handed the poor thing to Ashley and, before she could argue, she had a dog.

Sean was horrified. 'I am *not* looking after it!' he shouted as he stormed out of the room.

But this wee dog followed his footsteps. Ashley and I held our breath. The dog – her name was Honey – was chasing after him, we could hear her minuscule nails on the wooden floor. He came back in cradling her in his arms as she stared into his eyes. That was it – they were smitten with each other.

She slept on his chest; she lay on his knee. He sang show tunes into her face as he danced her round the room. He got her chipped at the vets, he paid to have her hernia repaired. Later on, she developed a blood disease and almost died and he paid thousands to save her life.

Honey changed our lives. We still don't know what age she is or how many pups she had, but we do know that so many people adore her. She ended up on a BBC TV series that Ashley was in called *Up For It*, and she became an internet sensation after I shared photos of her on social media and even made her 'speak' in my voice-over shorts that were becoming popular online.

Poor Honey couldn't walk far due to her miniature legs and past illness, so I suggested we get a pram. Once again, Sean was adamant that this would not be something that would happen, not on his watch. Anyway, Honey loved her pram and sat up proudly as she was pushed around the West End of Glasgow by a man who sang as he took her on long walks. Like I said, she changed our lives.

It was around this time I got my first shot at being on the iconic comedy news show *Have I Got News for You*, a programme I had watched for years and yearned to be part of. I arrived at the studio petrified, thinking I would die of fear at any moment, and carrying a huge case of imposter syndrome. Surely they would find out I was actually shite and kick me out of the studio.

Thankfully, Paul Merton and Ian Hislop were amazingly kind and welcoming; they made me feel very much at home. Despite me being so nervous that you could hear my skeleton rattling every time the camera panned to me, I did good – a clip of mine was even featured in their end-of-year show. I went on to make a few more appearances on the show and got some brilliant feedback – not from the usual right-wing trolls, of course, who demanded I be sacked and let me know I wasn't funny and nobody liked my comedy.

The online abuse had been getting worse over the years – the more popular and vocal I became, the nastier it got. I've always been a staunch ally and supporter of LGBTQ+ rights; I try every day to show solidarity with the community. The gender critical movement was soon being aligned in the press with Christian US anti-abortion far right groups who believed feminism was akin to communism. Trump supporters were against trans people, so that tells you all you need to know. I found myself frequently targeted by folk who openly opposed trans people. They mocked my mum's death, they made memes about the child abuse I suffered, and they spent days trawling through my socials making sure their feelings were loud and clear.

Thankfully my comedy audiences have always been very supportive of my stance – and when I went out on tour, every show sold out and people loved my work. It's as if what happens online isn't real life!

And it seemed my real life just kept getting better. I was actually nominated for the Groucho Club's Maverick Award for my Trump protest. It was a huge honour, and a really big deal as it's awarded to someone who's made 'an outstanding contribution to the world of arts' – I was up against Banksy, for crying out loud! I really couldn't believe that fighting back – and swearing – could take me so far.

After the success of *Wild Rose*, my acting career was really beginning to take off too. I hadn't landed a big role yet, but I did get a part in a TV series called *Traces*, a gritty crime drama based on an idea by Val McDermid. I jumped at the chance to act again. It was a relatively small part, but the show would be aired UK-wide. I got to act alongside a fellow west of Scotland powerhouse, Martin Compston, as his character's lawyer, so I was nervous nonetheless. A serious role in a TV drama was definitely a step outside my comfort zone – as I improvise so much in my comedy, the one thing I find difficult with acting is having to stick to a script – but I tried not to let my nerves get the best of me. It helped that everybody on the set – especially the director and the wonderful Martin – was incredibly supportive.

I felt I'd come a long way since my first foray into acting at the Fringe. I was certainly becoming less nervous and more confident with each job. After *Traces*, I went on to co-write and act in a wonderful short film.

It was a very unusual process. I was approached by the director, Fi Kelly, who had me in mind for the lead part in the project. The brief was tricky – it had to include a mermaid and it had to be about renewable resources. Fi and the other writers, Oliver Maltman and

Jules Middleton, asked me if I had any ideas, and how I would write the script. So, each of us writers jotted down an outline, and we sort of mashed our ideas together to come up with the film, which was called *The Last Mermaid*.

The film centred around a middle-aged Glaswegian mermaid, the last of her species, who has to figure out whether she wants to have a baby and save her race from extinction, or let her line die out. For me, a big part of wanting to tell the story was the fact that my mammy drowned. I wanted to tell the story of a woman who drowned, but came back as an important, worthwhile character. It wasn't the end of her life. That's what inspired me to write it, it was a kind of love letter to my wee mammy who never made it out of the water, I suppose. The last line of the film was, 'as my mammy said, if I can't be an inspiration let me be a dire warning.'

It was shot in the beautiful village of Luss on the banks of Loch Lomond, one of my most favourite places. I had so much fun making that film. I got to improvise a lot of the script while filming, which suited me, the cast was fabulous, and the story was hard-hitting but dead funny at the same time. My heart was the size of Govan when I saw the final product.

I couldn't believe it when our film was later nominated for six awards at the Scottish Short Film Festival – I thought it was an amazing film, but I did not expect it to do so well. And I definitely did not expect to win the award for Best Actress – that was an ultimate 'pinch me' moment.

I really loved being so involved in the creative process with *The Last Mermaid* – especially working as part of a team as opposed to being on my own onstage – so much so that I felt I wanted to write more. I had thought perhaps another play or possibly even another short film. But then I was approached by the publisher Hodder & Stoughton about writing another book. It was enticing. At our first meeting in their beautiful boardroom, I was being encouraged to write whatever I most wanted to. The trouble was I had absolutely *no idea* what the hell that was.

After our first meeting with Hodder & Stoughton, Chris and I went for lunch in Soho to celebrate.

'So, what are you going to write about then?' Chris asked.

That's when it hit me. I wanted to tell a story about the women I was surrounded with growing up, the Isas, the Buntys; I wanted to write a love letter to Glasgow. And it was going to be a murder mystery, the type of book I always loved to read myself. I love a good killing in a book. Now I was going to write one of my own.

157

15

I HAD NO idea how I was going to juggle my upcoming *Soup Pot* tour and write my first novel, but I was super excited nonetheless. It felt fitting that new milestones were coinciding with a new decade: 2020 was looking exciting. Of course, none of us could know what lay in store.

In late 2019, I was back in Glasgow on the day the news came through that my publishers also loved the idea for the novel. I had their go-ahead and Sean and I went into a local pub for lunch with Honey in the pram to celebrate.

The place was pretty quiet, so I got chatting with our server, a lovely young Irish woman called Caitlin. I asked her if she was studying in Glasgow and she told me she had recently graduated and wanted to work in publishing, or maybe even be a writer.

'That's fabulous, well done,' I said.

She seemed a bit despondent. 'Yeah, well barmaids don't always write books,' she replied.

'I was once a barmaid and I wrote a book, you can do it,' I said. Then I had a thought. 'Listen, I was just offered a book deal today, it's a novel and it's set in the seventies so I'm going to need a researcher to help me write it. Can I have your number?'

She looked at me as if I was a creepy insane person who wanted her number to stalk her. She had no idea who I was, but she jumped in with both feet too and we met up for a coffee a few days later. I explained the storyline and what I was going to need from her. I needed to get a grasp of the politics, music and culture of the seventies, so Caitlin had a job on her hands, as she wasn't even born then.

Something told me she'd be good though, and I like to trust my instincts. So I offered her the job right there. I knew what it was like, trying to make a career for yourself in a creative industry as a woman with no connections to fall back on. 'I'll give you a leg-up,' I told her, 'so that when the time comes when you're successful, you can give someone else the same.'

So with Caitlin on side, whenever I had free time I started scribbling down my ideas, developing characters, writing out a few pages. It was a daunting prospect, writing a novel, it was unlike anything I'd ever written before, but I was eager to get going and feeling hopeful for how it might turn out. Then something major threw a spanner in the works – for us all.

At the beginning of 2020 my *Soup Pot* tour had taken me up and down the UK to smaller theatres. I had a lovely tour manager, Trevor, who drove us all over the country and did my tech on the night. We stayed in Travelodges, washed our clothes in launderettes and ate cold sausages that we had purloined from the hotel breakfast in the car. It was smashing fun.

Trevor and I were in the car when the news broke on the radio that a virus was sweeping through China from Wuhan. I remember the moment so well.

'I don't think our King's Theatre gig in Glasgow will go ahead if this virus comes to the UK,' I said to Trevor. We were simultaneously scared and in disbelief that it would happen – we couldn't see a virus sweeping the globe, not in our day and age. That was a Hollywood film plot, not something that happens in real life, right?

Well, we all know what happened next – talks of quarantine, stories on the news of people dying, hospitals filling up, and emergency government meetings.

So many jobs had been lined up, so many gigs, more acting work, writing sessions in the Mitchell Library with Caitlin – it was all cancelled. The world went on hold.

In March 2020, on the day my King's Theatre gig was supposed to go ahead, the announcement was made. Lockdown – a word no one in the world wants to hear ever again. The news updates were more terrifying as the days dragged on; there was an overwhelming sense of national fear. I was worried sick – what if all three of us at home caught it and died and the sausage dog had to eat our rotten bodies?

For Ashley and me, being self-employed comedians meant we were on our own. Social media became the only way we could reach out to people; Ashley had to do her radio show from the bedroom, and comedy gigs were moved online, which was utterly awful at times. It is so difficult to perform comedy on the internet because there is such a delay, and that delay defies what comedy is – there's no audience interaction; you can't gauge how well it's going from how loud the laughter is. It was incredibly difficult. The upside to online comedy, though, is that you don't have to wear knickers.

Folk were living with extreme uncertainty, and it broke our hearts to think that so many people were on their own, isolated in their houses. So Ashley and I decided to do nightly livestreams to talk to folk, have a laugh, share our fears and bring some sort of happiness back into people's lives. We both had a good following on Facebook. It seemed like a good plan.

We had no idea how popular it would become – an incredible number of people joined in and chatted with us, we played games, we did comedy sketches, we had pop quizzes, we tried to make people feel less lonely. We even had special backdrops made so the living room became a studio. Most nights we had over 40,000 views. It became a global event; people from all over the world were tuning in with us.

At the same time the Scottish Government was doing daily Covid briefings, which could be long-winded and depressing. So, to lighten the mood, and help people understand what was going on, I decided to take all the facts from the live briefing and voice-over First Minister Nicola Sturgeon and her team to try to explain the ever-changing rules. At the end, 'Nicola' would shout, 'Frank, get the door' as she left the studio. After a while, it became such a popular catchphrase that I knew we could use it to raise some cash for a charity that's always been very important to me – the STV Children's Appeal. It helps local kids in small communities who are struggling. And I was one of those kids – I was a child who was starving, who went to school without shoes, who ate from a bin and looked into bakers' windows wishing I could have a pie. I teamed up with a brilliant merchandise creator, Ian Adie at Promotional Warehouse Glasgow, who created loads of 'Frank Get the Door' merch, including clicky pens. All the profits from these early sales were donated to the appeal.

These daily videos became viral hits all over the world. Nicola Sturgeon often retweeted them, which couldn't have been a better endorsement, and soon they were being featured across TV shows and mainstream media. So many people have told me, even to this day, that I got them through lockdown, making them laugh during the worst of times. I was very touched; I didn't feel I was doing anything special. I was amusing myself too, just sitting in my bedroom doing daft voices while other people were out there doing real life-saving jobs.

We wanted to help people as much as we could, so Ashley came up with an idea to do a twelve-hour Care-a-Thon for the charity Carers Trust through an online livestream. Lots of young people are carers for family members and this was a Scottish charity close to Ashley's heart. She has looked after her dad when he was ill, and her dad cared for my dad, all unpaid. She raised over £14,000 and stayed online for twelve hours straight (I merely dipped in and out of the broadcast). It was a huge success and we proved that online work can still raise awareness and help connect people during the worst of times.

It was horrifying watching local businesses shutting down, people losing their livings, everyone desperately trying to keep their heads above water. The internet became awash with Covid deniers, anti-vax people and some downright madness; it was hard to keep spirits up and maintain a healthy mental attitude – Ashley and I spent the majority of lockdown eating our feelings.

The only positive that came out of the pandemic was seeing people come together to support each other. My local Italian restaurant, Eusebi's, was my lifeline. Giovanna Eusebi, the owner, is a community-minded soul, like her family before her. I've known them for decades – when I was a wee girl, the Eusebis played a huge part in our community in Shettleston. We used to get our hair cut at Eusebi's barbers! It's lovely that that sense of community has stayed with Giovanna and followed the family into the West End.

Giovanna donates food to the homeless, and she prepared meals for those confined to their houses during lockdown. She became such a good pal during those tough times, and it was great to be able to sit outside with Honey in the pram and get a decent plate of pasta. Not that my waistline needed it; I was the size of a small manatee after the amount we'd been eating while stuck in the house. While most of the population seemed to be doing Joe Wicks exercises online, we were chomping our way through sweets and cakes. I tried exercising at home, walking round the flat with a sausage dog at my heels and annoying the neighbours by running up and down the stairs. It would have all helped if I had stopped eating bags of jelly sweets three times a day. It was a tough year for my waistline was 2020.

Trump was blathering on about drinking bleach and people were posting images of various politicians breaking the rules as governments across the world were scrambling to keep up with the virus. In April the global death toll exceeded 100,000 and, in the same month, Scotland's chief medical officer Catherine Calderwood had to resign after making two trips to her second home during lockdown. It was chaos.

To me, it felt like the world was ending. I couldn't see a way out of it, but I tried my best to remain positive and cheery. Sean, meanwhile, was in his element. I expected lockdown to traumatise him, given that such huge changes can be difficult for those with autism, but it turned out to be right up his street. You don't touch anybody, you don't have to go near people, you don't have to make eye contact: it was an autistic man's dream. Honestly, if the rest of his life was in lockdown I think he'd be fine with it. He really came into his own, and he was really helpful around the house, too, helping me organise my home studio for my voice-overs, stand-up, livestreams, the lot. He set it all up, he became the best grip boy/director ever! And I was glad for his support because working was the only way I knew how to keep going.

As a result of all the publicity, there was a huge surge in demand for my autobiography *Handstands in the Dark*. We were selling the books from the flat and from ten a month it went up to almost two hundred a week. It was hectic. The living room became a production line during the day, with the three of us signing, packing and posting out books. Then at night it was transformed into a studio. The nightly livestreams were still going strong and Ashley and I were creating videos for BBC Scotland, too. Plus we were both doing about thirty personal videos a day for people whose weddings had been cancelled, or for NHS wards, or people who couldn't celebrate their birthdays or make family gatherings. It made me feel useful that I could cheer people up at a traumatic time.

But I wasn't pleasing everyone. As the daily videos featuring Nicola Sturgeon got more traction, the keyboard warriors on Twitter got more riled up. They would harangue charities we worked with, and send screeds of abuse on Twitter towards any video we posted. Nothing was going to put me off though. I had bigger and better things to focus on.

When lockdown restrictions finally eased up later in 2020, Caitlin and I were finally able to get stuck into the novel, which was going to be called *Nothing Left Unsaid*. I would shout ideas for the characters across the study room we'd hired and Caitlin would write them down on a flip chart like Carol Vorderman. Caitlin not only worked on the initial research for it, but as time went on she helped me through the storyline and the process of writing it as well. It was all to be about sisterhood and struggle in the 1970s, inspired by the incredible characters I had met growing up in Shettleston and working in The Calton.

To help get us into the mood, Caitlin would dress in 1970s clothing and play seventies music as we sat down to work together. It was all brilliant for inspiring me, but I was still terrified. Writing my autobiography had been hard enough, but I didn't have to make any of that up. Now I needed to learn the skills of invention fast – and thankfully Caitlin kept me on track, because I was like a runaway train at times.

To make matters more difficult for myself, I was writing a dual storyline – a young single mammy's diary entries from the seventies, and her daughter's present-day life, which was complicated to pull off. But the most challenging aspect of writing was trying to keep tabs on all the characters, who swirled around in my head so much that they began haunting my dreams. I would text the long-suffering Caitlin at 2 a.m. for a who's-who of the multitude of characters. 'Does Bunty have two kids or is that Isa?' It was like I had a massive tangled ball of wool in my skull that Caitlin was helping me to unravel bit by bit. She is an absolute asset. Thanks Caitlin, when you read this bit.

I'm grateful that I was able to work and keep busy during such uncertain and terrifying times when so many people couldn't. I know I was one of the fortunate ones.

The pandemic even brought me the luck of meeting and filming with my hero Joanna Lumley, who was visiting Glasgow for her TV travel show, called *Joanna Lumley's Home Sweet Home – Travels in My Own Land*. But it was a close-run thing. On the morning we were due to film together, I woke up, got out of bed and almost fell backwards. I was so dizzy I couldn't stand, and I was due on set in twenty minutes. I was completely frantic. I genuinely thought I was having a stroke, but, as it turned out later once I'd been diagnosed, it was labyrinthitis, something to do with a David Bowie film and my inner ear. I didn't tell the crew I was feeling wobbly, so, when they asked me to sit on a rickety ancient bus and talk to the goddess on camera, I thought I might die every time we hit a bump. But I was determined to push through and luckily it turned out well in the end. Although to this day I can't lie on my right-hand side because I'm too scared I'll go dizzy and fall down another big dark hole.

My 'Frank Get the Door' videos got another boost when the people at the STV Children's Appeal asked me to team up with First Minister Nicola Sturgeon to make a TV sketch, in which she would actually say, 'Frank, get the door!' We had such a laugh doing it, and it raised thousands of pounds for charity. So I brought out a *Frank Get the Door* book in time for the world's first Covid Christmas, with a portion of the profits going to charity. We sold so many copies that we raised almost £50,000 all in for various Scottish charities. But despite the fact that the TV sketch and the book were a huge success, and I was doing what I could to help people in need, being involved with Nicola meant the online hatred surged and more than a few death threats were emailed to my website. Such is life.

Creatively, the pandemic spurred me on to do things I wouldn't have thought of before. Back in the spring I had landed a project that proved really tough, technically and emotionally. I was honoured and astounded to be asked by the National Theatre of Scotland to write a short piece of theatre reflecting lockdown. I screamed so loud when I got the offer that I frightened everybody in the house – including the dog.

I decided to go with an idea I'd had in me for about ten years, and wanted to adapt for Covid times. I called it *Alone*. It was a pretty bleak subject matter, about a woman who had been in a coercively controlled marriage for decades. It was going to show how the pandemic changed all the rules for her and her husband.

Technically, it was really hard to pull off. In fact, doing theatre and being directed through Zoom was possibly the most difficult thing I've ever done. But we all just started to adapt to challenges during Covid, didn't we? Even Sean – the man who never wanted to be involved in showbusiness – sat behind the camera and started telling me how to act. He even did all the lighting, too. Quite a lot of it was done with gritted teeth, but we got there.

There were four episodes, and it didn't take me long to write them at all, and it didn't take long to record them either. It was the bits in between – the rehearsals, the discussions – that were time-consuming. The longest part of it all was trying to upload everything online – I nearly threw my laptop out the window a couple of times doing so.

The pieces were recorded over two or three months, and we had weekly rehearsals. Aside from the first episode, which was a monologue, there was always me and one other actor on screen – Jack Lowden, Elaine C.

Smith and Joe McFadden – under the watchful eye of our director, Caitlin Skinner. My wee dog Honey even featured in the episodes and managed to steal the show every time, which didn't surprise me.

Filming *Alone* was a new process for me, but it was an interesting way to work and one that also played to my strengths, because we would only settle on a script after improvising. Then we would just go for it, but even when we did the final take we still improvised a little, because I can never stop myself doing that!

The first episode got 16 million views and, as far as I remember, across all four episodes we got about 50 million views. Each part received rave reviews online – it even made the national news. I couldn't believe the response. I was so incredibly proud. *Alone* became so popular that it ended up running as a series over Christmas and New Year 2021.

Along with the new year came a new chapter in my life – I was nearing my sixtieth birthday. Although the virus was still rampaging, somehow I truly believed it was going to be 'my best year yet', and I declared it on Twitter. If only I'd known what was really coming my way.

16

I CELEBRATED MY sixtieth just as the nation went back into lockdown. So, no party for me, though Giovanna and the Eusebi's team sent me a delicious three-course meal with a huge chocolate cake, all delivered to my door. Because I wasn't quite fat enough already.

The year started with a bang; my original autobiography *Handstands in the Dark* was reissued and released and started selling again, and I was still working flat out. I've always been the type of person to take as much on as I physically can, doing a hundred different things at once, but I'd noticed I was starting to feel more tired than usual, and I could see my appetite wasn't what it used to be either. I couldn't even finish Giovanna's delicious birthday treat for me.

Sometimes I was feeling a bit overwhelmed with doing so much: a weekly writing job with the Scottish newspaper the *Herald*; a weekly TV show for STV,

Talking Heids; still working on my novel, which was taking longer than I expected; hosting The Big Burns Supper event; doing the daily voice-overs; and hosting the nightly livestreams on Facebook. All this during lockdown, navigating jabs, masks and all the other Covid precautions we were having to take.

I returned to *Have I Got News for You*, with Covid screens separating the contestants. I still recall being driven through the totally empty streets of London, and staying in a hotel where they handed me a dry croissant for my breakfast. The memories of lockdown still haunt me and many others, although, on the scale of it all, I just feel lucky not to have lost any of my family to the virus.

Then I was offered a four-part TV series on BBC Scotland with Ashley, called *Janey and Ashley Get a Real Job*. Ordinarily, I would have loved it – the concept was fun and a bit ridiculous. It saw us travel about the country to try our hands at actual real work, from milking cows to putting out fires in an airport. But I was completely exhausted the whole time and I couldn't work out why, which made me worry. I felt really bloated, too – despite my appetite failing me, I was still huge around the middle. None of it made sense, so I didn't have a great time, to say the least.

But I carried on, as usual. My spring tour for 2021 had been pushed back to November because of Covid rules in theatres, but I was still so excited to get back onstage and to some form of reality. So when my agent told me I'd been offered the lead role in a panto in Aberdeen, I didn't hesitate to accept that as well. I had never done a panto before and knew I'd love it! I had no idea how I was going to fit it in to my already jam-packed schedule, but before I knew it I was being fitted for the outfit and having press shots taken, the scripts were getting assembled and I was starting to have meetings about my input to the show.

I was at full tilt, but the same seed of doubt was sprouting in the back of my mind – the nagging worry about my energy levels and my lack of appetite. Although I could hardly eat, I was still bloated like a manatee.

Here's something I have never really discussed before, but which helps explain my issues surrounding my weight. I have had eating disorders all my life; they came and went at different periods of growing up. When I was very small and suffering abuse, I simply stopped eating. It became a battle of wills to get me to eat a dinner and I think I lived on tins of creamed rice for a few years. In my teenage years, when Dad had left and my mum went off the rails, I was starving a lot of the time, and thankfully got free school meals, but some days I was so hungry I would eat thrown-away food out of bins in the school canteen. This bad relationship with food is something I have never really confronted, but it stays with me today. Bingeing and starving were a normal part of my life.

There was nobody who could convince me I wasn't fat when I was a young woman, despite my weight having stuck at around 8 stone 7lbs for most of my adult life on my 5-foot 4-inch frame. I had big boobs and couldn't disguise them, so I decided to starve them down. After Ashley was born, I was living on 300 calories a day. I was working full-time in a pub and looking after a newborn baby – how I never fainted and fell down that cellar I will never know. I would eat a Boots 'Crunch and Slim' biscuit for lunch and drink down some vile, gritty Cambridge Diet soup for dinner. I was starving myself but still I felt too fat.

I look back at photos from when I was in my twenties and can't believe how normal I looked; in my head I was obese. It wasn't helped by the many men in the pub passing comments. 'Oh, should you be eating that?' – this from a wee man who looked ten months pregnant watching me eat a biscuit. Looking back, I am genuinely astounded at how I never picked up a flame-thrower to the men in that pub who contributed to my eternal lack of self-esteem. And most of them resembled human Weebles, with trousers that never sat on their waist but were tucked under their huge basketball bellies. Why the fuck did I listen to them?

My difficult relationship with food was part of the reason I ignored my loss of appetite for so long. I just ignored the inner voice that was telling me to address my sore, bloated abdomen too. Something in the back of my head kept telling me to stop doing so much and address these bizarre symptoms. But I didn't. I put my swollen belly and exhaustion down to laziness, and carried on. The other bit of my psyche holding me back is my inherent fear of being poor again. Just the thought of it brings back all the feelings of being starving from day to day, waiting for a school meal to fill me up, or worrying that we won't have electricity, or being terrified of getting evicted and having nowhere to go. So, I work and work and try not to let anything get in the road of that.

On I went and organised accommodation for the pantomime in Aberdeen. I got all the rehearsal dates in place, which was vital as I would be coming off an exhaustive autumn tour of thirty-eight dates across the UK, finishing the novel, writing a weekly column and doing voice-overs before going straight into the panto. And I was recording comedy sketches for the STV Children's Appeal, too.

There was one other commitment I'd just taken on. It was to record an advert for the Scottish Government to encourage people to get the Covid jab. It got a lot of attention, but not for the right reasons.

I broke my own rule by taking the government's money. I'd always said I wouldn't do that – it makes you susceptible to a higher level of scrutiny if you take from the public purse, and quite rightly so. Taxpayers have every right to really know who their cash is going to.

I was filming for the STV Children's Appeal one evening when I got a call from my agent, Chris. 'Janey, look at that email I sent you,' he said. His voice sounded off. 'Are those tweets yours?' I opened the email. 'Oh my God. Yes,' I replied. I stared at my phone screen and felt sick to my stomach. Incredibly offensive tweets I had posted over a decade ago had been exposed by the Daily Beast, an American news outlet, and they were going to release the story in the press the next day. Chris warned me that I had better get ready for the onslaught. I was utterly gobsmacked and completely ashamed of myself.

You'll remember I mentioned that the online abuse directed towards me really began after I joined the campaign to support Scottish independence back in 2014. My penchant for holding my ground meant I was sniping back at all the death, rape and abusive tweets that came my way. I should have ignored them. I should not have heckled back. But I argued for years with them.

Many of them lost their accounts for sending me threats. I think I spent so long fighting with people online that I lost sight of what was right or wrong. Being so defensive was exhausting and ended up nearly driving my mental health into the ground. Being Janey who always fought back and being applauded for being tough didn't help the situation. I should have just blocked them and moved on.

So in 2021, when the tweets were exposed, all the Twitter trolls who had been wishing for my downfall for years had their big glory day at last. It had taken them years and many trawls through my social media but they were finally happy, they finally got me.

I looked again at the tweets, which came from back in 2010 and 2011, when I was commenting on *The X Factor*. I'd been sitting at home bitching about what was on telly that night. Now I was absolutely horrified at myself. They were disgusting. Some of the comments I wrote about a woman of colour were utterly horrific and inexcusable. And they were still up on Twitter for everyone to see. They were far back on my feed, but they were there.

What the hell was I thinking? I guess I just assumed that because I was openly on the left, because I had protested against racism and marched against fascism for many years, people would know I wasn't racist. But

179

that's not how it works – that's not a good enough excuse. It wasn't comedy or 'freedom of speech', it was hurtful, sloppy, racist language from someone who thought that being an outspoken comedian put them above criticism.

You can't use that language and hurt people and expect them to forgive you. I know that. You have to accept when you are wrong and apologise immediately. When the tweets hit the news, it was a shock and a struggle even for me to understand and explain. It was all my fault. So I wrote an apology and made a video, which I posted on all the social media platforms.

My world turned upside down. The Scottish Government dropped me from their campaign and had to make statements regarding their reasoning for hiring me, and a TV show I was working on was put on hold. I was dropped from the panto too. I donated my fee from the government to the STV Children's Appeal, who also dropped me from their campaign.

Within hours of the story first breaking, all the UK newspapers and social media outlets were writing about me. From then on, for weeks, it was all over social media daily. I had to close my Twitter account and come off Facebook.

I want to be clear at this point: I had no one to blame but myself. They were my words; this was my issue and

I had to deal with it. I could also see there were some double standards, as our prime minister at the time had also said some awful things in the past. But that doesn't get me off the hook for saying some really shitty things.

The daily onslaught was horrendous. I just thought every single day I was going to get an email to say, 'we've found another thing you said'. I stayed in my bed, I couldn't see anyone, I refused all my friends' calls. I wanted to die. Gigs were cancelled and I was facing losing my tour. I'm so grateful that my agent was always incredibly supportive; he was just trying to make sense of the Scottish politics in the background and at the same time make sure my mental health was being looked after. I was supported by thousands of people who wrote to me as well, and my neighbours and friends all stood by me. My husband and my daughter were utterly devastated at the fallout; we discussed it extensively and they supported me as best they could. I was numb with fear and shame. I also had to accept that having argued with mostly men online for years was something I needed to address. It wasn't healthy, none of it was healthy in fact; it was all a fucking mess.

17

I DECIDED TO end my life. I couldn't face another day of the *Sun* having a go and they weren't ready to stop. Every day they sent an email to tell me they had found another thing I had said that was offensive and they were going to print it. I had had enough.

I couldn't see an end to the pain so the best thing to do was end me. At 5 a.m. I walked into the ensuite toilet and worked out how to throw a bathrobe belt over the shower rail and see whether it could take my weight. I sat there on that toilet pan thinking about what I needed to do before I went, like taking care of any bills. I remembered I owed American Express £56, and as if on autopilot stood up and went through to the living room to organise sending through the payment. That simple, everyday action was exactly the thing I needed to alter my train of thought. I was no longer only thinking about myself and I realised I couldn't take my own life and leave my husband to find my body. Imagine what that would do to Ashley too?

So I found myself calling the Samaritans, who spent a good hour talking me down off this proverbial ledge. They helped me to find a way out of the anguish I was in. They saved my life.

Thank God for Amex, the Samaritans and £56.

In the days that followed I talked to a friend, who advised me to get emergency counselling online, which I did. It was the best cash I have ever spent. My therapist made me face up to the fact that I had spent too many years arguing mostly with men who mostly didn't matter. She helped me realise that I didn't have to fight any more; she helped me learn how to stop. Which – after so many years of battling to be heard, to be respected, to stand up for what I believe in, to make something of myself – was no small feat.

Most importantly, therapy helped me find the strength to save my own life. I began to address the child abuse I had suffered, and why feeling shame is such a trigger for me. I have always suffered with shame – the shame of being the poor girl at school with dirty socks, nits in my hair, probably smelling like sperm because I was being abused by my uncle. I felt shame every day. It's something that sets off the worst feelings inside me, and it's what sent me into a spiral of depression.

That's the strangest thing about therapy, the way it digs up things from the furthest corners of your brain that you've tried to hide away. In my first emergency therapy session, almost as soon as I opened my mouth I started talking about when I was in Glasgow city centre, a few days before Christmas in 2014, getting presents for Ashley.

Just as I approached George Square from Buchanan Street, I saw the flashing lights of an ambulance. When I got closer, everything felt quiet, although it couldn't have been. I froze. There were bodies scattered over the road. I remember walking backwards and thinking, I can't look at this. I went into the newsagents and asked for a bottle of water. He said there had been an accident, and it sank in that something terrible had happened. It turned out that a bin lorry had crashed. Fifteen people were injured; six people died.

I wanted to help, but I didn't know how to, so I posted on Twitter to say there had been an accident and to avoid the area. Immediately, the press started calling me, but I couldn't cope with that. So I walked down Queen Street to stop people coming near with their prams and kids, because the Christmas carnival was on and I didn't want anyone to see what I had seen. I can't quite remember what happened exactly. But I remember walking for four hours, I couldn't stop.

And then I went on *Channel 4 News* that night to talk about what I'd seen. But I didn't tell the whole truth. I couldn't – my brain had blocked it out. I'm still getting therapy for it now, and I don't think I'll ever get over that.

It's the same with the cancellation, I can't fully remember details of that day. I was told your brain protects you from remembering the worst things too clearly. Even the memories you do have can be unendurably painful. When I wanted to end my own life I thought maybe it was the right thing to do because I'd forget everything bad that had ever happened to me.

While I was trying to heal old wounds from my past, and process what was happening in the present, I stayed quiet on social media and instead tried to focus on getting myself ready for my upcoming tour. Despite the letter-writing campaign by the Scottish Tories that had succeeded in losing me the panto, none of the theatres cancelled my shows.

The online onslaught was continuing though.

My agent Chris and my family were my rock during this time. They encouraged me to get back out there and make people laugh. I didn't want to go on that tour; I have never felt so dispirited about doing comedy in my life. I couldn't imagine anyone wanting to come see me after the very public shaming I had brought upon myself.

But they gave me the confidence – and they were proved right. As soon as I announced I was doing it, the entire tour sold out.

Standing behind that familiar black curtain on that first night in Arbroath, I cried silent tears. I felt so shattered and couldn't imagine bringing any joy to even one of those people in the audience. When the lights went up and I walked out onstage, my stomach was in my throat.

I couldn't believe what happened next – the crowd were on their feet giving me a standing ovation even before I opened my mouth. The roar was overwhelming. The support made me break down and cry. I apologised from the bottom of my heart at the top of each show for what I'd said on Twitter.

That first show went amazingly well, as did each one that followed. It was utterly soul-restoring to get back out onstage after so long in lockdown and then being cancelled. The audiences reassured me I hadn't lost my fan base out there. Brilliant as it was, I couldn't stop feeling shaken and I still wasn't mentally or physically robust. It was a tough time, but ultimately there was no one to blame but me.

The tour went all the way down through England and into London and back. Each show was getting great reviews, but anyone who saw it and wrote about how much they enjoyed it was being hounded on Twitter by men who disagreed with me politically. You weren't to like me or say anything nice or you would get a pile-on. My fans were being trolled but they stood strong. The irony was, many of the accounts on Twitter who were calling me racist had timelines full of racism and anti-immigration right-wing rhetoric. That's politics for you. Now, I ignore them. I've spent too many years fighting back.

All the positive feedback boosted my mood, and the tour itself was also the huge financial boost I needed after so much fallow time. The blows of losing the panto and some private corporate shows were now behind me as I focused on the rest of the tour.

Offstage, I was still working on the finishing touches to my first novel, and continuing with therapy to work on my mental health. Therapy was helping me feel a little mentally stronger, but physically I felt exhausted most of the time, and I could hardly eat anything. I was surviving on about 400 calories a day, as I tried to lose my ballooning fat belly but feed myself as well. One night in London, after a brilliant show with a standing ovation, I was buzzing, but felt exhausted. I knew that I was due to go to dinner with my agent Chris, Don Ward from the Comedy Store, and the team from the Groucho. I really wasn't feeling well. They all set to with huge

plates of food, whereas I could hardly manage a couple
of wee sausages.

Chris clearly knew something was wrong and took
me aside. 'What is going on, are you ok?' He was visibly
concerned and I explained I was just emotionally drained
from the whole cancellation ordeal. Poor Chris, I can't
imagine what it did to him – he must have been rinsed to
the bone as well from managing all the media fallout.
All those years ago when he signed me up he must have
thought, 'A wee middle-aged Scottish comedian, what
can go wrong?'

As the tour continued, my tour manager Craig was
equally worried about my energy levels and pointed out
that, when I was onstage in Aberdeen, I'd been rubbing
my upper leg and stomach.

'You need to get that looked at, Janey,' he insisted. I
didn't know I was so visibly in pain that people could
see me struggle. I promised him I would go see a doctor
when we got home.

I put everything I was experiencing down to stress.
Until I saw a tweet by the TV presenter Julia Bradbury,
who was explaining the symptoms of ovarian cancer, as
she was dealing with her own breast cancer at the time
and was aware that women weren't always checking for
obvious signs. My stomach lurched and I went ice-cold.
Suddenly, everything made sense – the bloating, the

needing to pee constantly, feeling full all the time, not being able to eat. Fuck.

Could it really be cancer? As you'll know if you've been paying attention from the beginning, the answer, sadly, was yes.

18

AND SO IT was that within a single day I found out I had an 11-centimetre tumour in my abdomen and Covid to boot. I had really hit the jackpot. Well done me.

I was scheduled for an urgent hysterectomy but, because of my Covid infection, I had to be discharged from hospital and wait seven weeks before it could happen. So, I took my giant watery belly and my 11-centimetre ovarian tumour and headed home for the wait.

Both Ashley and Sean were infected with Covid, too. They were gravely ill and couldn't stop coughing, but I was bizarrely unaffected – other than having cancer. I basically had to nurse both of them as I tried to take in my news. Just as well the panto had been cancelled – well done those Scottish Tories on their foresight.

It was awful to see Sean and Ashley so sick, but it did take my mind off the whole cancer thing.

Telling Ashley was the hardest thing I had ever done in my life. It's like throwing a hand grenade into your family and hoping they survive the fallout. We knew nothing really about it, I had no idea what to expect and kept thinking I was going to die in a few weeks' time. I visualised the tumour and called it Bunty, while trying my best not to get angry at people who kept telling me to 'Fight on' like this was a fist-fight and I could just punch the cancer out of existence.

That's the biggest misconception about cancer – that it's like you're actually in some sort of boxing ring going up against something you can beat down. I know I've been a fighter my whole life, it's part of who I am. I could understand people thinking, 'Janey's a battler! She's battled all her life! This is just another that she'll win!' But that's not the case. This isn't a fair fight.

There isn't anything you, as a patient, can do when you have cancer. Cancer, to me, is all about hoping your body deals with the chemicals and surgery and the disease doesn't spread enough to kill you. You don't have a say in it. There is no bravery or strength, no winners or losers. You basically give your body up to science and hope that it can withstand what comes next. Don't get me started on the people who contacted me online to sell me pigeon juice as a remedy. Or the bampots who told me that big pharma have a cure for cancer but just won't share it out. People loved to tell me about all the cures for cancer they knew about. 'Like sucking off an owl?' I would ask, just to see their faces contort with anger.

The online trolls of course told me I got cancer due to karma, which raises the question, why do babies get cancer? But I had to stop fighting back with them and leave it to others to deal with their hatred.

The Scottish NHS were amazing; they set me up with a Zoom meeting with the surgeon and she gave me all the details of what to expect and talked me through the whole operation, as well as what would happen after – probably chemo, depending on the pathology. I wanted them to talk to me plainly; I wanted to know all the details.

So, my hysterectomy was planned for early in the new year. I was utterly petrified. I had never had an operation before and I was terrified of anaesthetics. What if I couldn't walk up our stairs after the operation? What if I died on the table? Fears were flooding through me in waves.

That entire seven-week wait for surgery was purgatory. It was like time stood still. I didn't want 6 January to come because I was terrified of what would happen, but at the same time I was desperate to get the tumour out of me. It was a nightmare.

Sean, Ashley and I spent that Christmas time feeling so subdued, the three of us round the table: me trying to eat while I listened to all the fluid squishing about inside me; Ashley in near-constant tears; and Sean trying his best to be cheery. We tried not to think that this could be the last Christmas we would have together, but it was constantly in the back of my mind. Trying to have a positive mental attitude is bloody hard. It annoys me when people keep saying, 'Stay positive' – I want to hit them with a shoe. People need good news, so they keep projecting that onto me, but I just wanted them all to stop offering 'positive affirmations' and accept that I am dealing with the worst news ever.

Giovanna down at Eusebi's was a blessing during this awful time. She was constantly dropping off food for the family. So, to say thank you for her continued love and support – and to cheer us all up – some pals and I organised a surprise flash-mob choir to assemble outside the restaurant. My pal Chris Judge, who is an amazing professional singer, turned up with his bandmates and choir and we had a lovely Christmas sing-song. We all joined in, we sang, we laughed, we cried, and we drank good coffee. It lifted my spirits more than I can say. That was when I realised that good pals would be the secret to my strength through this cancer ordeal.

My pal Shirley decided that after the operation I would go and stay with her to recuperate. She had a spare room, she was practical and organised, and she would do anything to help me. Also, she was desperate to feed me; Shirley is a great cook and a feeder, and she knew I hadn't eaten much in months. So, the room was prepared and waiting for me.

At last, the dreaded day arrived. At 7 a.m. Sean drove me and my packed bag to the Royal Infirmary, just east of Glasgow city centre. The sun wouldn't be up for over an hour; the dark sky was ominous, and it was also absolutely freezing. To make matters worse, Covid rules meant that Sean wasn't allowed to come any further than the hospital entrance. I was terrified. I clung to him, crying – I didn't want to let him go. The nurse had to peel me off him. I felt like such a pain in the ass, but I was just so scared. I turned to watch him walk away as they took me in to prep me for the operation and inserted the first cannula of many into the back of my hand.

I was the first hysterectomy of the day. I was shown into a small room and told to strip off, pull on compression socks and sit on my bare arse on a plastic seat until the anaesthetist, called Gavin, came in. It turned out he lived near me, and was a fan of my comedy. 'Did you ever heckle me?' I asked.

'No, I'm not stupid,' he replied. I trusted his judgement.

Gavin and a few nurses took me into another small room before I went into the operating theatre. Gavin told me to sit on the edge of the bed and bend over as far as I could. This wasn't something I was prepared for, but I did my best. 'What's going on?' I asked.

'We are going to insert a small painkilling rod into your spine,' he answered as I felt my left leg go numb and the rest of my body tingle.

'That feels weird—' I started to say as they laid me back down, and I was about to launch into a lengthy conversation, but Gavin pushed the drugs into my cannula and, for the first time in my life, a man shut me up. In seconds, I was out cold.

Hours later, I woke up on the ward, covered in wires and tubes and looking like spatchcock chicken. There were women across from me and beside me and beeping machines that never stopped. I would have paid a thousand pounds an hour for the beeping to stop. Trying to sleep in a busy ward with minimal staff and a plethora of noisy machines was utter hell. But I was alive and that was all that mattered. I had a tube draining my bladder, a tube in my stomach with a wee bag filled with pain relief, oxygen up my nose, and a drip in my hand and more wires that sat on me like a pile of spaghetti.

Out of the chaos all around me, the care assistant, a wee Glasgow woman, appeared at my side. 'Ready for a shower Janey?' she asked softly. I looked at her, aghast. She must be joking; how could I possibly shower? I was hooked up to machines and bags. What was she thinking? But without hesitation, or waiting for me to respond, she went into my bag, got my toiletries and marched off. She zipped back and – how, I will never know – got me out of bed and upstanding. She carried every single attachment that hung from me and guided me to the shower room at the end of the ward. My legs felt like hollow cheese strings, my head swam, but she kept me walking. She was about five foot tall but she had the strength of an oil rigger and was blessed with the patience of a good granny.

I cried in the toilet. 'I can't get my gown off round all these tubes,' I sobbed.

Within seconds she was a blur of hands and instructions and, in no time at all, I was naked and shivering and crying in a shower. Like a baby. She gently washed my back and gave me a cloth to do the front. I have never felt so grateful in my life as I did for that wee woman. I was handed a towel and dried most of my body. She sat me down, dried my feet, pulled those awful compression socks back on, got me into my pyjamas and brushed my hair. I sat there completely exhausted, thanking her profusely for her kindness. She just said, 'Brush your teeth hen.'

I did as I was told, only I used a tube of Clarins moisturiser instead of toothpaste, in my state of confusion. We both laughed so much. She got me an NHS toothbrush and toothpaste and we started over. Then, on stronger legs, I walked back to my bed. Whatever they pay those care assistants, it isn't enough.

Back in bed, feeling cleaner but still very dazed, I texted my family to let them know I was ok. I knew that the surgeon had spoken to them earlier, when I was in recovery, to tell them how the operation had gone – that was arranged before I went into theatre. I still wasn't allowed any visitors, but to be honest I was glad. The last thing I wanted was to see anyone; just the thought of reassuring people or making small talk made me feel ill.

I was lying there exhausted and barely able to keep my eyes open, but not in pain at least, when the surgeon – who was tall and businesslike – came in to tell me that when she opened me up, she'd noticed the tumour had burst inside me during the seven-week wait. She didn't use flowery language or innuendo to soften the blow, which was great because my brain was too fuzzy for that. Straight to the point, as though she was giving directions to a park, she explained that she had removed my womb, Fallopian tubes and ovaries, and that she had noticed some 'gravel' on the tissue surrounding my womb, so she had she cleared some of that away. I always wondered where the gravel in your knees from childhood scrapes went to when the scabs healed. She reassured me it wasn't that kind of gravel.

The surgeon then explained that they had drained three litres of fluid from my abdomen, which explained the pain that I had mistaken for heartburn. No more Gaviscon tablets needed then, I thought, and briefly wondered if the company would go into liquidation as I had spent thousands on indigestion remedies.

The hospital encourages you to eat, but after my first mouthful of hospital food I immediately started vomiting and couldn't stop. Let me tell you that retching as your stomach muscles clench after a major op is no fun at all. Yellow acidic stuff filled the papier mâché hats the nurses set in front of me and I felt like I might die.

The ward was insanely busy and staff were stretched thin. A nurse decided to give me an anti-sickness drug through my cannula to help stop the puking. As soon as it entered my veins, I felt the strangest blood-fizzing rush. The nurse looked at my monitor and I could see the panic on her face as my heart rate started to rise. I could feel banging in my chest and everything went blurry. I was having a reaction to the drug. She quickly whipped out the syringe from the cannula and tried to calm me down. I felt as though I had done fifty lines of cocaine and was running down Argyle Street naked in the rain, being chased by a rabid Alsatian (I have never done cocaine but I have been chased by a dog). The effects soon calmed down, in time for me to vomit more.

The vomiting wouldn't stop.

The surgeon explained I had an ileus, which sounds like a tragic Greek play about a woman who is chased by a dog and can't stop being sick. It meant that my stomach wouldn't let the gastric juices pass through and they needed to be drained by putting another tube in me, this time a rubber one that went up my nose and down into my stomach.

I can't tell you how horrific that procedure was. Unluckily for me, they got it wrong and I managed to vomit round the throat/nose tube, so they had to rip it out and start again. Two nights of trying to vomit and swallow round a rubber tube. Everyone else in the ward was getting out of bed and leaving the hospital whereas I was stuck with big jammy plasters over my face holding a rubber tube in place. I felt so sorry for myself.

I naïvely believed this was the end of it all – I had cancer, they removed it and now I could go back to work. I knew so little about the disease, and, no matter how many books and pamphlets you're handed, you still can't grasp the enormity of it all.

Eventually the nurses removed the tube and I finally stopped vomiting, so it was time to leave the hospital.

Shirley came to collect me and we had a meeting with the surgeon before I could be discharged.

That room will stay in my mind for ever. There was a print of some pastel flowers on the wall, a small Ikea table covered with advice books on cancer, and a peach carpet. It was like that room in a funeral parlour where you buy a coffin. Shirley arrived and we sat holding hands, trying to be brave and stoic. The surgeon sat down opposite us. Her expression was sombre.

'It's stage 3b cancer,' she said. Straight to the point, again.

Shirley gripped my hand tighter. 'What does that mean? Can it be cured?' I was trying to stay calm as the panic swelled in my chest.

'No, it can't be cured, but it can be treated,' she replied.

'So, there will be no "all-clear"?' I asked, my voice shaking.

The doctor shook her head. 'No.'

She told me there would be chemotherapy and treatment until . . . well, they didn't know when. Nobody knows what's going to happen next. Ultimately you just keep pumping chemicals into your body, chasing the cancer round and round until one of you gives up. Well, that was going to be the case for me. I would never be cancer-free.

201

I really can't remember much of what happened next. All I can picture is that the exit to where Shirley's car was parked was right beside the Promotional Warehouse, where all my 'Frank Get the Door' merch was made.

It was so surreal, standing there, just numb. I had to call Sean and explain the prognosis. I asked him to call round all the family – I just wanted to go to Shirley's and sleep. It took us a while to get all the way to East Kilbride from the hospital – first Shirley had to stop crying before she could manage the 20-minute drive home. Neither of us spoke that whole journey. When we arrived, I walked up her stairs into the room she had prepared for me. She quickly took off my coat, helped me into my pyjamas, and put me into bed.

Silence, no beeping monitors, no women crying, no traffic noise. Just wonderful silence.

The next few days consisted of Shirley jagging me with blood thinners, making me walk up and down her hallway to help with my bloated torso, and feeding me. I still can feel the joy of eating a roll of corned beef and coleslaw with a big mug of tea. It felt like I hadn't eaten properly in months, which of course I hadn't. The litres of squishy fluid in my torso had put paid to that. I honestly don't know how I managed to record a TV show with Ashley and go on tour with awful dull abdomen pain and a big ovarian cyst sitting inside me, slowly spreading its cancer cells round my body.

On the fifth day Shirley got me into the shower and, without warning, ripped off the big sticky bandage that covered my belly. Only a best pal can stand you naked and rip off your surgical dressings, and Shirley was that for me. She patted me dry and got me back into bed and ready to go home after a week.

Sean, Ashley and Honey were at the door, excited to see me – Honey most of all. She was frantic and screamed as she ran about as fast as she could manage with her tiny legs. Her personal feeder had been missing, but now said treat-giver was back!

Sean and I prepared for the next step in my treatment, because there will always be a next step. I was, and am, very aware there will be no all-clear. I had to keep making this fact known on social media – it seems it's the general assumption that you get treatment, ring the all-clear bell and live out your life, being grateful that you've come through it. That wasn't going to happen for me. I would be dealing with cancer until it finally killed me. That was a fact I kept trying to make clear to the press, who always want a 'good happy ending'.

I was also doing my best to raise awareness about the symptoms of ovarian cancer, using my huge social media platform. Even still, the abuse from the trolls continued.

They suggested I was lying about cancer; they would send tweets asking me to die quicker. But a huge tsunami of love and support drowned them out. That annoyed them, I'm sure. Although I had bigger things to worry about.

Chemotherapy was the next stage in this entirely unexpected journey.

19

THE CHEMO WAS fucking hard.

When the day of my first session arrived, Sean and I packed a bag and set out at 8 a.m. for the Beatson cancer clinic in the West End of Glasgow. I had put on so many charity gigs in aid of cancer survivors at the Beatson – I never once thought I would be a patient there myself. I had no idea what to expect, I just knew I was going to get a drip, go bald and vomit for a while.

The Beatson do such great work. The hospital is amazing, and the place is bright and airy, not cold and scary like most hospitals. When I got there, I was quickly attended by a man named Brian, my chemo nurse. I got all my vitals done and he explained what would happen with the infusion protocol–the steroids, the antihistamines and the chemo. I cried my eyes out once again. I could see women and men walking past the room, really slowly, bald and weak, and all I could think – selfishly – was,

'Please don't let that be me.' I knew it would be at some point, of course, but I couldn't face the fear of that. Ever since I was a wee girl, I'd had a full head of thick curly hair. And I was strong on my feet. I couldn't bear the thought of the transition into exhausted and bald. Although that would soon change – it's amazing how your priorities switch when you are trying to stay alive.

After the cannula was inserted, I was given the steroids and antihistamines and then I was to have two different chemo infusions, names I can't spell or pronounce. The day went slowly. The chemo nurse kept a close eye on me, as you can have a profound reaction to the drugs – I didn't know this at the time and wondered why he sat with me for a good while. Thankfully, there were no weird feelings as the chemo went into my body, I just kept needing to pee. I quickly learned how to unplug the wheelie thing that holds the drugs, make it into the loo and pull down my knickers without dislodging the cannula in the back of my hand.

Brian spoke to me about my hair. 'You should think about getting it cut short so when it starts to come out you won't have it falling all over the house in big strands,' he explained. It was a good idea, but I secretly believed my hair wouldn't fall out. Because I am naïve.

The days following the chemo were horrible. I wasn't sick, but I had such strange, random pains throughout my stomach during the night. I called the cancer helpline and they advised me to attend the Royal Infirmary emergency room. It was a Saturday night in Glasgow, so Sean and I sat for hours like everyone else with the short smatterings of police-and-drunk-people theatre vignettes breaking up the boredom.

Eventually, after an examination and a scan, the doctors came to the conclusion that they didn't know what was wrong. So they gave me some painkillers and sent me home. But I was given an appointment to see the surgeon who had operated on me. She's incredible.

'You know how you have taken away all my giblets and bits, what is left up my vagina?' I asked her. 'Can you look up it like a toilet roll tube? What's at the top?'

She laughed. 'No,' she said. 'We tie it up at the cervix like a stump.'

So, now I have a wee fanny stump.

The inexplicable pains finally receded, and luckily I had no vomiting or mouth ulcers or heart attacks or any of the things I googled when I was lying in bed worrying myself into a fear froth. I did get some good news. After I was diagnosed, I found out that there was a test to see if your cancer can be passed on to your kids. I can't tell you how relieved I was to hear that my genetics proved the cancer will not be inherited by Ashley. We both cried our eyes out that day. We also learned to take each win as a gift from then on.

After a few sessions of chemo, the inevitable happened – my hair started to fall out. So Ashley and I decided to video her cutting it short. I wanted it to be fun, not traumatic; I wanted other people to see it's not the end of the world.

The response from people from all around the world was unbelievable – people I've never met were sending me hats, knitted blankets, prayer cards, gifts and so many other lovely things. Their generosity was overwhelming. I will NEVER forget all the love and support from strangers during this time.

When the time came, Sean shaved my head. Strangely, I wasn't apprehensive; I had just accepted that this was what had to happen. I took a really touching photo of him holding my chin in one hand as he shaves my head with a razor in the other. I shared it on Twitter, knowing the press would pick up on it. I wanted to show people going through the same regime that being bald isn't the worst thing.

When the remaining hair fell out and I was completely bald, it was so bizarre. I would sit up in the middle of the night and look at myself in the mirror and think, Fuck, is that actually me? It's really weird when you look out of your own eyes and see everyone around you and think you look the same, or a certain way you imagine, then when you see your real reflection in a mirror it's quite a shock. But there was something brilliant about being completely bald. Some people suggested I should try wigs, but I didn't want to wear a wig, or a wrap. I just wanted to be bald. And then my eyelashes fell out, then my eyebrows all fell out, and then I had the smoothest legs I've ever had in my entire life. People kept saying, 'God, how are your legs so smooth?' Chemo, that's how.

One thing nobody warned me about is when your hair starts to grow back in it actually hurts. It's genuinely painful, like sunburn. Now I realise when people say babies are grizzly, it's probably because their hair's growing in.

But feeling the summer breeze on my head was oddly amazing after years of having hair like a Shetland pony and a big sweaty scalp. It took six minutes to shower and I have saved thousands on hair products and maintenance since. I didn't realise my hair had been such a big part of me until it was gone. It felt good to know that I actually had a personality, and I wasn't just my hair. That was cool.

The chemo continued, and it wasn't easy. Walking back down the corridor at the Beatson, bald and weak, I saw a young woman in a side room staring at me with fear in her eyes. I wished I had walked in and told her not to worry, we all get weak and baldy for a while.

The worst part, for me, was the steroids. I have never experienced such a range of emotions – not even with the menopause, although I'm sure Ashley would tell you different. One minute I would be seething with rage, the next I would be depressed, scared, anxious. It was hell. I was still on chemo when it came time to launch my first novel, *Nothing Left Unsaid*. I managed to make my way around Waterstones book shops across Scotland to sign copies. I was so proud; there was so much love poured into that novel, and my publishers had been amazingly supportive while I dealt with cancer and chemo. They just kept propping me up and urging me to go on.

I was aware how badly the whole cancer thing was affecting both Sean and Ashley. Because they have autism, they don't always cope with grief and fear in a traditional way. At one point Sean had a breakdown, at just the point when his psychology appointments had been stopped without any notice. Of course it was incredibly distressing, but I also knew millions of people were suffering mental health issues after Covid and no government agency was able or willing to help finance the problem.

It began slowly – he would snap at me for asking him a question, or simple dialogue would somehow become a huge explosive argument. He started to go silent for hours at a time, aside from a few mumbles, refusing to make any eye contact at all. He began to either sleep too much or stay awake for days. His moods could be triggered by anything I said and for a while he refused to talk to me. It was a pattern I had seen before and I was deeply worried. I was trying hard to keep myself emotionally stable – I knew if I shed one tear, I would completely fall apart.

My husband was shouting at the TV, refusing to eat, and one morning he woke me up at 5 a.m. to tell me he wanted to die. He was angry at me, he explained, for saving his life when he was seventeen years old. Back in 1980, I had realised he had taken tablets to end his life, so I'd rushed him to the hospital. He was blaming me for making him live this life – I should have let him go, apparently. I was gobsmacked. I couldn't believe he could say something so ridiculous. 'Well, we can't go back and change things now!' I yelled. 'Just like I can't go back and change having cancer or getting cancelled! We have to deal with what's happening *now*!'

With Sean's NHS psychotherapy cancelled and him refusing private treatment, I had nowhere to turn. It was a terrifying time – I had no idea how to cope with his emotional wellbeing as well as my own all at the same time. I was completely overwhelmed.

Finally, we ended up spending a whole night talking it through. It seemed to calm him and we tried to muddle on as best we could, but I knew he needed professional help.

Ashley was deeply anxious and juggling working on her weekly radio show and filming a TV pilot. On multiple occasions, so as not to worry either of them, I would secretly call the cancer helpline and not let Sean or Ashley know what was going on. It's a fine line to walk when you are showing side-effect symptoms and trying not to worry your family. I did that many times. Not telling them was my way of dealing with it. We were in our toughest times yet.

Whenever I updated my social media to explain what was happening with my health, the press would use the photo and the tweet and make a news story out of it. I was becoming weekly clickbait and getting abusive pile-ons from those suggesting I needed the press to keep writing about me for sympathy, when in fact the press were just lifting from my social media posts. Eventually my agent, Chris, asked them to stop. It took a couple of days, but they did.

Chris was as amazing as ever. He dealt with the cancellation with great grace, and now he did the same with the cancer and the fallout of having to refuse work while I was in recovery. He reminded me that we had a

tour starting in February 2023, so we decided to call it
Not Dead Yet – it suited my sense of humour.

I was still getting regular chemo and at the same time
recording the audiobook of my novel. It was hard, to
say the least. The chemo affected my throat and voice,
so some days I sounded like a squeaky frog and others I
was talking like my Uncle John, who smoked sixty
Capstan Full Strength on a daily basis. Thanks to help
and understanding from Nick the producer and the rest
of the studio, we got through it slowly. We postponed
when my voice was bad and I turned up when my throat
was fine. People were so considerate and patient with
me. It's amazing when you have that much support, it
props you up; it stops you feeling like an invalid 24/7.

The people who treated me at the Beatson were just
amazing; every three weeks they took such good care of
me and, even when I left after five hours, I had the
24-hour cancer care helpline to turn to if and when
things went pear-shaped. They're always on hand to talk
you through your worst fears and send you to A&E if
needs be, which happened a few times when my
temperature spiked. The concept of 'too much
information' goes out the window, too – those poor
women at the cancer care know more about my bowel
movements than anyone has a right to. It's never a dull
moment with chemo.

Every day you learn a new way to cope with the side effects of whatever treatment you're on. The steroids I was given made me foam with anger and lose my temper with everyone and it ravaged my mental health. The irony with chemo is that it saves your life and poisons your body at the same time. Living with the constant fear of something going wrong is exhausting, but somehow I was getting through it.

20

WHEN THE DUST had settled a bit, I felt ready to talk about everything that had happened in such a shockingly short space of time. In fact, I was desperate to speak up. So I agreed to do an interview with Bernard Ponsonby, a current affairs correspondent, who asked me to do an exclusive with him for *Scotland Tonight* on STV. We were to discuss the cancer, the cancellation and the new book. To say I was nervous was an understatement. Bernard really went deep about the effects of the historic tweets and the abuse that ensued. But it was a relief to finally discuss it out loud.

Although, as I decided not to wear a hat and instead go bald on telly, the overwhelming support I got was offset by the mockery from trolls, who made cruel memes and sent them to me. But all that contrasted with what I saw in real life. Whenever I was sitting outside Eusebi's, strangers would stop almost daily and tell me, 'You got me though lockdown, I wish you well,' which was so kind and reassuring. To this day, not one person has come up to me in person and said anything abusive. Another reminder that Twitter is not real life.

In March, I was getting stronger but I wasn't strong enough to do the King's Theatre show, which had finally got the go-ahead. And I wasn't allowed to be around so many people, because being on chemo jeopardised my immune system. Instead, we decided to put on a new show with Ashley hosting in my place and a brilliant line-up of Scottish comics, who were devoting their time for free. One hundred per cent of the profits would go towards the Beatson Cancer Charity – we raised almost £43,000 through ticket sales, merch and buckets on the night. I am so very grateful and proud of every single person who showed their support that night, especially the performers who came along to do their craft for free. I really do have amazing pals.

Alongside feeling weak, my side effects from chemo were a loss of taste buds (I started eating really spicy curries just to actually taste food), failing eyesight (I needed glasses), neuropathy (my toes and fingers went numb and tingly), and no hair anywhere on my body. My skin felt like glass, too. Oh, and the backs of my hands were ruined with cannulas, but I didn't want a port inserted into my chest; I felt that would be something else I would need to constantly deal with. So, the nurses and I carried on playing 'hunt the vein' in my hands every three weeks at the Beatson.

I finished those rounds of chemo in late spring, and a CT scan was booked soon after. A few weeks later I got the results. I was indescribably happy when they showed 'no evidence of disease', but I had to keep reminding people that I wasn't cured – that would never happen. My chemo specialist Sharon was always very honest about the long- or short-term outcome. I would not live without cancer and I wouldn't have as much time as I would have liked. But the press especially kept misrepresenting my social media updates, so I had to keep on making it clear that I would not survive this. Which can be very depressing to read, I know, but I wanted people to see the real face of cancer and the effect it would have on me.

In response, some people would say things like, 'Nobody knows when they will die, you could get hit by a bus tomorrow!' I wanted them to be hit by a bus today. I was sick of hearing people contemplate 'how long life is' – they could all fuck off. I just wanted plain talking and honest support, no platitudes.

As I always did when times were hard, I used humour to deal with this whole fucked-up car crash in my life. Like when my lovely pal Jason Manford – who is such a fabulous comedian and friend – came to Glasgow and we made really dark jokes and laughed at cancer.

It was Ashley's go-to coping mechanism, too.

'Ashley, please make me tea.'

'Can't you make it? Oh, that's right, you have the bad, bad cancer. I'll make you tea.'

There were nights when Ashley and I laughed so much. 'Mum, what if the cancer just clears up,' she said once, 'then folk will really think you faked it.' We laughed even when we felt like crying, when I was weak and completely exhausted. We had to carry on.

There's a cycle with chemo. The first week you're tired, the second week you feel a bit better and the week before the next session you start to get exhausted again. So you work out the cycle that suits you, when you can leave the house and get some exercise. Whenever I was able, I would walk with Sean and Honey in the pram – sometimes I could get up to five miles a day. Most days, I would pull on a beanie hat and head down to Eusebi's, and Giovanna would fill me up on home-made soup and love. Watching people go by as we sat drinking good coffee with Honey in the pram was a great antidote to the doom and gloom inside my head.

Despite the energy-sucking, bald-making chemo, I was still being creative, and missed being onstage. I got the chance to do a BBC Radio 4 special called *Janey Godley: Still Got It* with the awesome team of Richard Melvin and Julia Sutherland at Dabster Productions. I was so happy to be working again, and happy to be able to get out of the house more often, too. It was recorded at Websters Theatre in the West End of Glasgow in front of a live audience and they put a chair onstage so I could sit down when I got too tired. My comedy pal big Scott Agnew was my support on the night, and the show went amazingly well. It was the first time my fans had seen me onstage since the cancer diagnosis, and they all cheered when I walked out. It's important for me to keep mentioning how much love and absolute support I was given during the darkest moments of my life. Honestly, I was overwhelmed by people's reactions and grateful for all the love they sent me.

The next step in my treatment was a course of pills called PARP inhibitors – a fairly new drug designed to stop the cancer cells growing, to give patients a chance to live a relatively normal life after chemo. Every week you have to have blood tests and blood pressure results before you get the tablets, as they can affect your haemoglobin and therefore your bone marrow. Which is not good. The doctors were also keeping a close eye on my CA-125 number (the indicator that the disease is active).

The tablets were harsh on my body, I felt extremely exhausted after taking them and often couldn't make the stairs up to my flat. There are fifty-five steps from the close to my door – those stairs were my daily workout – but before long I was having to sit down on the landings in between flights as I couldn't make it up without a rest.

One month during a consultation, Sharon explained that my blood count was so low they couldn't let me leave the hospital and I needed a transfusion. 'I don't know how you're upright – you must be exhausted! Do you feel faint?' she asked as she booked me into a bed. The PARP inhibitors were bleaching out my haemoglobin – I'd always known it was a possibility.

That blood transfusion was amazing, I felt like a VAMPIRE. Honestly, I could have run up a mountain afterwards! We kept on with the PARP inhibitors, but my blood tests were showing that my CA-125 was creeping up slowly but surely – not a good sign. It's completely terrifying to have your life and sanity dictated by a number in your blood. Sharon told me to wait until the scan in October before we worried too much, but she did say that it wasn't good news. She never once airbrushed the truth.

Then there was another issue – I developed a hernia, which appeared like a fat baby's head poking out the side of my belly button. I've had a scar above my belly button since I was two as I developed a hernia when I was little, but it hadn't ever affected me. This one was painful and was triggered by things like eating bananas, porridge or sticky rice. All the things I like. There is no cure or operation I can have – they don't want to risk opening me up again – so I have to wear tight vests and big tight elastic belts that wrap round my middle. This, added to the many scars and bald bits, has unfortunately disqualified me from any future beauty pageants.

21

TWENTY-SEVEN YEARS, UMPTEEN weeks of chemo and one major surgery since my first show, in 2022 I headed back to Edinburgh for the Fringe.

It was a special time for me. It was my first bit of alone time in over three years, and I was itching to get there. I wasn't able to put on a full gig, but I could go through by myself, see my pals, and do some slots on other shows. I stayed at the Moxy Hotel Fountainbridge, where the staff knew I was alone and gave me some reassurance that they could help me if needed. Ashley and Sean were worried about me going away on my own, so this really gave them peace of mind. Me, the woman who had travelled all over the world doing comedy all by herself, now needed support for a few days in a city forty-five miles away. But I shut my mouth and enjoyed the freedom from hospitals, scans, blood tests and needles.

I guested on a few podcasts and some chat shows, then spent time on the stunning roof garden of the Moxy, overlooking the sun-soaked rooftops of Edinburgh. It was strange that some people didn't recognise me with no hair except for a wee smattering of white pixie down on my scalp. I had to say, 'It's me, Janey!' to a few comics who stared at me blankly when I first spoke to them. I could see the shock on some of their faces, but it was just good to spend time with my comedy mates. Everyone was so supportive and glad to be out of lockdown and back onstage – the positivity was infectious.

I returned to Edinburgh a week later for the book festival. There was to be an event for my novel hosted by the journalist Ruth Wishart on a rainy Monday morning at eleven. I was sure nobody was interested – after the cancellation and the cancer and stuff online, who the hell would want to come and see a greety woman who wrote a book? – so I didn't even bother to check the ticket sales. The venue was a brown sandstone church hall near Tollcross where I had often stayed when I was doing the Fringe. I had walked past this old windowless building opposite a nightclub for years and had never noticed what it really was.

Inside was HUGE! Like a Tardis. I was flabbergasted when they showed me into the auditorium, such an amazing space with windows all around the enormous dome in the ceiling above. I was even more astounded by the turnout. We had sold 800 tickets for the event – the place was heaving.

I enjoyed the event so much; it was wonderful to talk about my novel, which was really a love letter to my mammy and her pals and Shettleston where I grew up. The audience were so engaged and excited. I will never forget what a wave of love it was.

It made me think back to the chilling moment in 2021 when I'd nearly taken my own life. I was so glad I didn't. For every single person sending me hatred and abuse online, telling me to kill myself, there were hundreds more sending me love.

Focusing on my health was all that mattered now. I needed another CT scan to see what was going on, so at the end of August I headed up to the 'scan in a van', which was basically a caravan with a scanner in the car park of the Queen Elizabeth University Hospital in Glasgow. I was extremely nervous and weepy, but this is everyday life for people living with cancer. You basically cope from scan to scan and hope the cancer goes into some form of hiding. I know it exists, still, inside me, I just don't want it to become active and start spreading around my organs.

The scan is pretty easy; you get a needle inserted, which delivers a dye that is pumped around your body and makes you feel like you need to pee. This is just before you are inserted into a giant doughnut scanner that tells you to breathe in and out. It takes about two minutes, but it feels like time is suspended. Then you carry your bra and clothes in a bag, boobs flapping about in your jumper, as you run out of the van back into the hospital to get changed.

There is nothing to alleviate the scan anxiety. But you have to learn so many skills going through cancer – one is learning that worrying doesn't change the outcome; another is trying to live each day normally, not expecting too much of yourself. I was still working, doing some radio shows and appearing on Lorraine Kelly's morning television show, speaking out about ovarian cancer to raise awareness.

Thankfully, the scan was clear again, but the bad news was that my CA-125 number just kept rising, so that was all going to hang over me till the next scan in November. That's basically how it goes, scan-worry-scan-worry-scan and worry. The good news is, the Maggie's Centre up at the Beatson has great counsellors who can give you time and advice when it all feels overwhelming.

One day after a meeting with Sharon the cancer specialist, I walked up to the Maggie's Centre, which is on a hill, exhausted and weeping. There at the main reception was a lovely man who just walked me into a room, made me a cup of tea, held a hankie for me and let me cry for about twenty minutes without saying a word. He listened to all my fears, my worries, and never told me everything would be fine, he told me that I would cope in a way that was best for me. He let me rant and snot all over his lovely room – it was open-plan and spacious, with floor-to-ceiling windows and a view of the garden outside – and made me feel just that little bit better. The best thing about this meeting was that I got to organise for Sean to see their resident therapist to help him cope as well. That came at just the right time. I can't thank Maggie's enough for their patience and care.

I'm lucky that I was able to keep my mind busy with work – I was actually launching two books about Honey. Yes, my wee sausage dog had two fun books, one for adults and one for kids. Honey was a big part of the voice-overs during the pandemic and became very popular. Unsurprisingly, she was the star of the show when the book launch at Waterstones came round. A lovely crowd of Honey fans gathered and my comedy pal Susie McCabe hosted the event as my wee dog wandered about the shop looking cute while barking at people.

All through this period though my blood count kept dropping, which meant I needed another transfusion, and the CA-125 kept creeping up and making me feel sick every time I got results from my weekly blood tests. The PARP inhibitors made me feel washed out, so I could no longer go on walks with Honey in the pram, and I was getting frustrated and angry with Ashley and Sean. But I had booked a week's holiday in Ballater with my pal Monica and her sister Elaine. I've had a timeshare cabin there for over thirty years and always love it. Monica and Elaine are like sisters to me, too; I have known them both for over twenty-five years. They packed all the food and drinks we would need for the big cabin and drove me up through the beautiful Cairngorms, where we stopped to take in the stunning views – the huge mountains, big blue sky and vast open space that makes you realise how small you are.

I was eager to get to the cabin and settle in with the girls, but I could hardly walk up the steps to the lodge. Elaine pretended she was tired too, but I could see from her face that she was worried – she could never hide her feelings; her big blue eyes always betrayed her thoughts. Elaine was my walking pal; we used to walk the two bridges in London from Putney Bridge to Hammersmith Bridge, round Barnes and back to Fulham. Now I could hardly make the three steps into the lodge, and struggled even more with the eight steps inside the house up to the living room.

Monica and Elaine fed me up and drove me into Ballater every day (we used to walk it). In all the time I've had that timeshare I've rarely met anyone as I mainly stayed in the lodge or went swimming in the hotel next door. But Monica and Elaine went into every single shop, spoke to every single person, looked at every single bit of art, touched every single bit of cashmere, stared at every whisky, chatted to the local butcher and made friends with every dog they met throughout the village.

I knew they were devasted by the cancer diagnosis, but we still had a wonderful time. They bundled me up in warm clothes and we had a walk in the rain. I sobbed. I used to be able to manage these walks easily, but this time I felt like an old woman. Monica and Elaine managed to lift my spirits and took me for a swim in the pool next door.

I love being in the water. The pool was perfectly quiet and the weightlessness was brilliant for my hernia, so I had some relief at last. But nothing could stop me worrying about that scan result to come. I knew the results couldn't always be clear – especially after the CA-125 rising from 56 to over 200.

When I got back to Glasgow, I immediately needed a blood transfusion as my haemoglobin had dropped again. Those PARP inhibitors were draining my bone marrow. I was trying hard to stay strong and get ready for my tour in February 2023, but I was also starting to see the likelihood of that not happening. I didn't want to let everyone down; the theatres had been booked, the equipment had been hired and the tickets were selling out.

Now, almost a year after I was diagnosed with ovarian cancer, I was back in hospital getting another blood transfusion. Lying in the ward getting blood pumped into me, I could smell hospital food drifting from the wards around me; I could hear the all-too-familiar sound of beeping machines, and the clip-clop of Sharon's heels coming down the corridor. She's the only person in the Beatson who doesn't wear soft shoes.

She swished the curtain round my bed and I knew by her face she didn't come bearing good news. I took my glasses off and put my hands over my face. 'Should we get Sean up here to discuss the scan results?' she asked gently. That was when I knew it was really bad news.

I cried silent tears. Sean came around the curtain, ghostly white, and sat beside me. He gripped my hand and his own eyes filled with tears, too.

Sharon explained that the cancer had returned, low in my abdomen in front of my bladder. The PARP inhibitors weren't working. We sat in stunned silence. Eventually Sean spoke: 'How long does she have left?' he asked.

Sharon explained that there was no exact science, but they were going to try more combination chemo to see if that stalled it. There were no clear answers but we were aware that this might be the beginning of the end. Whatever that meant. When they'd both left the room I lay in that bed and bawled like a snotter baby. A wee woman in the next bed came over, swished open the curtain, held my hand and said a prayer over me. Religion isn't my thing, but the peaceful, graceful words helped calm me down.

I called my pal Tony Kelly from the visitors' room and we chatted for a while. Tony was the guy who talked me into being a comedy promoter at Wild Cabaret. I became firm friends with him and his family; he's like a brother to me. He's always been there for me.

Then I spoke to Shirley, Monica and Elaine. My tribe were there to lift me up, time and time again. I spoke to my sister Ann and tried to be brave; I FaceTimed my brother David and we both cried on that call. It was just devastating to see people hurt because of me and this fucking illness. Having to tell Ashley the cancer was back and active was utterly crushing. She was recording her show for BBC Radio 4 in Edinburgh at this point – how she managed to go back into the studio and keep her spirits up was beyond me.

Sean rang around the rest of our close circle to explain what had happened and deliver the awful news. All my friends and family were devastated, especially when we had to warn them that this news would make the press. When it did, I was sent so much love, support and goodwill from all my pals and friends in comedy, but straight away the trolls released their vitriol, wishing me a quick and painful death. I was too numb to pay attention and by now had stopped fighting back; I just let them rumble on and scrolled past. The sheer amount of support from pals on Twitter makes up for the madness you see on there.

I came off the PARP inhibitors and was booked in for more chemo before Christmas. We all cried buckets that whole week. My agent Chris was worried sick about me. It didn't help that the tour was only five weeks away and I didn't know if I could do double chemo and travel all over doing comedy. But I didn't want to cancel at this point, I just wanted to believe I would be ok.

So, we faced yet another gloomy Christmas. I kept thinking I was going die any day. This time the chemo was every week for three weeks then one week off. I was suffering with neuropathy in my feet, I was exhausted and my bloods were low. My hair started to fall out again and my eyebrows disappeared; my nose hair vanished and was replaced with a bloody scab that kept sporadically bleeding.

Everyone was trying their best to keep my spirits up, but there was no way I could face another gruelling round of chemo and keep smiling.

Eventually the decision had to be made about the tour, and I spoke at length with Chris and my family. I decided to cancel, do the chemo and spend 2023 recuperating and waiting to see how long I had left to live. We would wait and announce it when the theatres were through the panto season and able to cope with all the admin of a cancelled tour.

Before then, I was due to appear on the New Year episode of BBC Radio 4's *Loose Ends*. *Loose Ends* is one of my favourite shows and, despite the terrifying reality I was facing, I couldn't wait to get back out to work to do this one engagement at least. My old buddy Elaine C. Smith was on the bill, and I was so excited to catch up. Elaine had been such a rock during the whole cancer thing, taking me out to lunch, texting me regularly to see how I was, and we could talk the slippers off two pensioners at the steamie.

Another invitation arrived that I just couldn't refuse. In the middle of December I was invited by Jimmy Carr to Edinburgh for afternoon tea and a chat. I took Shirley with me and set off to the capital at the busiest time of the year to meet my pal at a fancy hotel.

'Let's have a wander through the Christmas market,' I suggested, which was possibly the most idiotic decision of my life, other than agreeing to get married into the Storrie family as a teenager. Every single street was HEAVING with people, lights flashing, hot dogs sizzling, prams battering your ankles and music blaring. The crush of people was terrifying – especially after being so isolated during and after lockdown, the surge of people was just too much. Shirley and I grabbed each other's hands and bashed our way out of the crowds, almost getting killed by a tram as we spilled out onto Princes Street. Obviously, it was just as busy there; thousands of happy Christmas shoppers thronged every bit of space on the pavement and the bus stops had huge crowds blocking the way.

I thought I was going to faint; I was used to a busy Edinburgh during the Fringe, what the hell was wrong with me? I felt so vulnerable and weak, my energy levels were fucked – just as well I had decided to cancel the tour, it was only weeks away and this was how I was reacting to crowds.

Finally, we made it to the Balmoral hotel. What a beautiful sight; the whole entrance was festooned in Christmas lights and a huge tree stood centre stage. The smell of pine and cinnamon filled the air. My eyes pricked with tears as I found a chair near reception. Maybe this would be my last Christmas, I thought. Shirley was on high alert. 'You,' she said pointing at me, 'enough of the weeping, or I'll join in.' She produced the ever-present bottle of water from her big bag and handed it to me to get a drink. Shirley had everything in that bag, from antihistamines to anti-bac wipes, and even a thermometer to check my temperature. I don't know how I would have got this far without her. The spacious hotel was an oasis after that hysterical mob outside. Fuck the Christmas market, never again.

On wobbly legs I made it up the stairs into the lovely palm-ensconced, cool tearoom and we were shown to our banquette.

It wasn't long before Jimmy joined us. With a warm hug and an 'Are you dead yet?' joke, we sat for a good hour reminiscing and chatting about cancer and comedy.

The afternoon tea at the Balmoral is utterly magical; we were talked through an extensive list of tea choices and presented with three layers of fancy sandwiches and delicious dainty cakes. We all sipped gracefully out of our delicate china cups.

'Why are you going to cancel the tour?' Jimmy asked, with his famous eyebrow cocked up at an angle.

'The cancer is back . . .' I explained as I stuffed a tiny cream cake into my mouth.

'The cancer will never leave. Is your mouth still working?' he replied.

'Yes, but I'm worried I'll be too weak to do an hour onstage,' I said.

'Fuck that, wear a hat, take a seat with you and get out on tour. Trust me, you will survive it and it will keep you alive – what are you going to do? Sit at home and cry?' he answered.

I looked at Shirley, she nodded and there and then I decided to carry on with my *Not Dead Yet* tour. Thanks Jimmy.

Up to the end of the year I had chemo weekly, with an added dose of antiangiogenic, which changes the blood vessels already feeding the cancer to make it hard for it to survive. I was finally looking forward to 2023 with renewed hope and strength. If I was only going to last a year, then I was going to make that year work.

22

EARLY IN THE new year, I surprised Chris with the news that I'd changed my mind. I now wanted the tour to go ahead.

He was over the moon, but nevertheless worried about my health and stamina. I assured him I would be fine and that I really, truly wanted to do it. We had countless phone calls and meetings about what to expect; we liaised with the Beatson, who managed my weekly chemo dates around a comedy tour and even gave me a blood transfusion the night before the first show.

Lying in that hospital once again with blood being dripped into me was the first time I really accepted what was happening to me; I faced that I had full-on cancer that would eventually end my life. I pulled the bedcover over my face and cried quietly. I was never brave. I felt sorry for myself every single day of this shitty disease.

Sharon the cancer doctor came to check in on me and wished me well on the tour. I was so scared I would fail. But it was a done deal now, the tour had sold out, so it was time to get ready and get off my sad arse and be funny.

Sean saw us off, Shirley got a bag filled with supplies and was on standby to deal with any medical emergency, as she had all the numbers and contacts for the Beatson. The winter sun shone brightly as we made our way to the first show in Arbroath, and Ashley and I sat quietly in the car with Chris, who had come up to see our opening night. Ashley was my opening support act; she also helped me remember my material, as my chemo brain was kicking in and I kept having memory blanks.

Just before the tour began, I had been approached by Hopscotch Films about filming a documentary that would follow my life on tour while dealing with cancer and all the ups and downs that came with it. I really wanted to do it, I wanted people to see me getting chemo, I wish I had seen people getting chemo and their honest reaction before I walked into that ward. I wanted people to see me being me and doing my best to have fun and enjoy my life.

Now, in Arbroath, we were meeting with the director/ producer John Archer and the camera crew to talk through the filming plan. Ashley and I went for a walk down to the beach after a lunch of Arbroath smokies and big mugs of tea.

'You ok Mum?' she asked as the wind whipped my surviving bits of hair about my head.

I took a deep breath of the bracing, salty sea air. 'I'm worried I won't be funny and my energy will fail me,' I replied.

'Ma, you can never not be funny,' she said with a smile.

That opening night is one that will stay with me for ever. Both of us were incredibly nervous as we stood backstage. We were about to go on when a montage of photos set to really sad music came on the screen onstage. There were photos of me and Ashley when she was young, photos of me just married . . . it was incredibly emotional. It was all Chris's doing and he needs his arse kicked – I hadn't seen it before. Naturally, Ashley and I were sobbing our eyes out. All I could think was, they're going to fucking show this when I'm dead, aren't they? I loved it though.

Then the music faded and I had to go out and open the show, and introduce Ashley, with snot and tears running down my face. I walked onstage to see the whole room on their feet cheering and clapping for me. I sobbed again; this isn't what comedy is supposed to be, all this crying and no jokes! So, I pulled myself together and thanked everyone, cracked a few jokes and brought Ashley onto the stage with me.

We both had a great gig. It was such a relief to be able to talk about the past year, laugh about everything that had gone on and feel strong enough to do such a big show. It felt really natural too; Ashley and I never rehearse our comedy; we do develop a sort of skeleton script but we mainly just make it up on the night, so it's still fresh every time. I like improvising onstage but it can mean the show will overrun. Every now and then Ashley would hiss from the side of the stage, 'We've overrun by forty minutes, Mum, get off!'

Chris and I had a big hug at the end and Craig, our wonderful techie/tour manager, and I breathed a sigh of relief. Craig had been with me on the previous tour that I'd had to cut short due to the cancer diagnosis; he'd been a stalwart during such a tough time – we all adore him and his ability to smooth out any techie issues that arise. I have an incredible team behind me.

The film crew caught everything. It was strange having a camera following us about, but it will all help to make it a brilliant, insightful film.

Arbroath was over two nights, but Ashley had to go back to Glasgow to do her late-night radio show on BBC Scotland, so we had my pal Scott Agnew, a wonderful award-winning comedian, step in as my support for the Friday-night show. Yet again we both saw the opening montage and stood at the side of the stage and cried buckets; this was going to be something we did for the entire run. That sad montage at the top of the show had everyone crying. And Chris needs his arse kicked again.

The shows everywhere continued to sell out, the reviews were amazing, and each night was another standing ovation. My energy levels were holding up, I was getting weekly chemo and still jumping in the tour bus to go onstage that night. Jimmy Carr was right, what was I going to do? Sit at home and cry? Nope, I was going to go out there night after night and make sure everybody had a good time.

People had come from as far as the USA and Canada, plus all over the UK, to see me on tour and Ashley and I were loving being on the road and getting to be funny again. The weekly blood tests and chemo did take their toll, but somehow the sheer adrenalin of being onstage carried me forward to each town. I wasn't dead yet and I was embracing it.

The day we were in Aberdeen for the tour was the day of the press conference that Nicola Sturgeon held to announce her resignation, so immediately I was back on to making a voice-over video to be included in that night's show.

241

I'd forgotten how much people really enjoyed the voice-overs, and doing them live in front of a screen was just utterly brilliant; I could improvise a lot more and swear even louder.

The tour was so uplifting. I forgot that the cancer had resurfaced and just kept working and kept up my chemo treatments to counteract the disease in my peritoneum. I might not live as long as I wanted to, but I will live *as* I want to, and comedy has helped me do that.

The tour also helped Ashley; she no longer had a wee frail mum at home sleeping all day waiting for the cancer to consume her body – she had a fully functioning mammy back onstage bathing in the laughter. And this helped us all as a family. Sean was over the moon with pride at our attitude, going back out there to do what we did best.

Soon the tour arrived at the Glasgow SEC and we had sold out 3,000 seats. I was so nervous; a home gig is always good fun but this one was HUGE. Honey was coming onstage with us and we had five cameramen and a whole tech crew backstage. Food and nibbles were brought in from Giovanna at Eusebi's as we were having a drinks party afterwards.

The whole day was taken up with tech rehearsals. I was staying close by at the Moxy Hotel (thanks for the rooms, Victoria) and Shirley literally dragged me back to the room, made me shower, took my phone off me and tucked me into bed for a nap. I was like a kid on Christmas Eve. I couldn't wait to see all the people who had supported me through the cancellation, the cancer and the ongoing treatment.

Sean brought Honey down to the SEC in the pram for her stage debut. 'Have you seen the queues and crowds out there?' he said.

'Yes, three thousand people are here to see her,' Chris replied proudly.

My heart was in my stomach. What if I just couldn't be funny tonight? What if this was the night I literally died onstage?

We were doing backstage interviews for the documentary crew, there were film crews out front, and we could hear the audience coming in through the speakers. My nerves were jangling as Shirley was serving tea in the green room. I could hardly focus on what was happening until we heard the techie tell us it was time to go backstage and get ready for the show. Honey was in her pram, bemused by all the attention and noise. The plan was that I would go out and welcome the audience and introduce my favourite daughter and Ashley would walk on in a mood pushing Honey in the pram and walk off again. It was a silly gag but I wanted the crowd to see Honey onstage.

My best pals were all there in that audience: Monica, Elaine, Elaine C. Smith, Tony and Claire Kelly. Sharon my cancer doctor and Rhona the surgeon who operated on me were there too. I was buzzing, I couldn't wait to get out there. It was the biggest venue I had played for my own show.

The lights went down and the funeral montage, as I called it, went up with the evocative music playing. I could hear people react to this by either clapping or sobbing, because that's what you need at the start of a comedy show!

Then I took a breath, smiled at Ashley and walked on. My legs were shaking.

The whole of the SEC erupted into one huge wave of love and applause; I was gobsmacked. The audience got on their feet and cheered even louder than I'd thought possible. I burst into tears. I had to gulp them down and get on with the show.

Everything went well. I brought Ashley and Honey on – Honey stole the show, as per usual – then we had Ashley do her stand-up and she stormed it. At the interval my stomach was still in knots. Shirley made sure all the lovely food from Giovanna was ready for our party afterwards, and Chris had organised the booze for the occasion too.

After the break I went back on and sat on the sofa to do the live voice-overs, which were projected on the big screen behind me. Everything was going brilliantly to plan until I stood up and drank some water.

Immediately, my throat closed and I couldn't breathe. I have never experienced it before, but my throat wouldn't open to let any air in, you could hear me struggle to breathe. I had inhaled the water instead of drinking it and I was dry-drowning in front of 3,000 people and a camera crew. The audience at first thought I was stumbling about as a joke, then they saw me gasping for air, and Ashley ran onstage with a big bottle of water. She was deathly white. She grabbed my back to support me and whispered, 'You've overran by forty minutes,' and I laughed. That helped me cough it out. She took the mic and said, 'It would be really awkward if this is how she dies . . .' and the room let out a sigh of relief and laughter as I coughed and managed to get my voice back. Sharon my cancer doctor told me later that she, Rhona the surgeon and Elaine C. Smith were ready to make their way to get up onstage to rescue me. Elaine said she would sing a song as they did CPR!

I can laugh about it now, but it was petrifying. Ashley helped me get my voice back, checked I was ok, held the mic and I managed the singalong part at the end of the show. So thanks to my daughter and my techie, Craig, I managed to get offstage alive. But I was so worried that I had spoiled it for everyone by nearly choking to death on a gulp of water; I was devastated that I almost ruined my big night. Thankfully, afterwards everyone reassured me that what I thought was forty minutes of choking to death was only 160 seconds in real time. When I saw the video later, I felt better – the show was brilliant. Although it took me a week to drink and swallow without fear after that incident.

After the show all my pals were there, having a glass of wine and some delicious food. Everyone was over the moon for me and equally terrified that I almost choked in front of them. When I tweeted about it the press yet again picked it up with the headline 'Janey Godley almost chokes to death', which was good enough clickbait for the haters, who soundly wished me dead again. But nothing could take away the love and happiness that gig at the SEC brought me.

The next day, I was back at the Beatson getting checked out and getting more chemo. My hair was falling out again and I still had scabby nosebleeds, but it was time to head to London.

Craig got the car ready and we set off. Lots of pals were coming to see the show and have a wee final tour party. The journey down was fabulous; we sang songs, played music and tried not to distract Ashley, who was writing scripts for a new TV show she was going to be filming in August. But Ashley can sing songs, dance, stand on her head and write a script at the same time. She's always been multitalented and a multitasker. She had just appeared in a pilot for a TV programme called *Dinosaur*, about a woman dealing with being neurodivergent, and the show had been picked up and was going to be shot in Glasgow with Ashley in the lead role and co-writing. We were all so proud of her. I was ecstatic – I needed her to have something to focus on instead of my long-drawn-out cancer baloney.

Going to London to end the tour was my way of controlling my own life for a while, and a three-night sold-out run was enough to pick my spirits up.

Ashley and I were staying at the Groucho, and we had the best time. It was like the old days when we would come to Soho, eat in our favourite ramen restaurant, walk round the cafes, drink coffee outside Bar Italia and people-watch in Soho Square. I do love London so much.

The Leicester Square Theatre is just amazing, the staff are so bloody good at what they do and, although I had sour memories of standing backstage looking at my swollen belly not eighteen months before, trying to work out what was wrong with me, I felt fitter and stronger than ever standing on that stage with my daughter. The shows were a triumph; the turnout was amazing. Even my wee pal Brian from New York flew over to see us.

Brian works in TV over there; he and I became pals over Twitter and he had come to Glasgow to see a few of my shows over the years. It was such a joyful experience – how I desperately needed those good vibes!

On the last night we held an end-of-tour party at the Groucho where my mate Jonny The Fizz organised a table, food and a huge magnum of rosé. Elaine, Ashley, Craig, Brian and I had a fabulous time, singing, drinking and celebrating the fact that we had finished a sold-out tour with me and my terminal cancer.

23

I DIVIDE MY life into before cancer and after cancer.

Before cancer, I would walk for miles up the Maryhill canal with Sean; we would run down the wee hills and try to make a five-mile walk before lunch. We would count the swans and their cygnets, take photos of them for Twitter and relish the fact we were both middle-aged yet fit. Once we walked all the way to the Erskine Bridge from my house, along the canal side – fifteen miles. It took hours, but we were determined to make it. Both of us were exhausted, legs aching, and we had to get a bus back home, where we soaked our feet in hot water, laughing at our madness.

Before cancer, I would pick clothes I loved without having to worry that they would stretch over the massive post-operative hernia that I have beside my belly button.

Before cancer, I didn't have to work out how many stairs I would have to climb in a venue before I got to the green room. Many times on the latest tour, I sat on an uncomfortable step backstage because the dressing room was too far away and I didn't want to exhaust myself before walking on. It was easier to just be close to the stage, even if it did mean a sore bum. I was privileged enough as an able-bodied person to never have to consider how people with physical disabilities ever got onstage. Now I check theatre websites to see if I need to bring a cushion to sit somewhere close to the stage entry.

Before cancer, my feet, toes and fingers weren't numb due to nerve damage.

Before cancer, I didn't have to lie down after I ate food to help ease the hernia.

Before cancer, I didn't need to check the veins on the back of my hand to see if they would survive another chemo infusion.

Before cancer, I had hair that fell down my back in thick golden waves that cost a fortune to maintain and broke at least three hoovers by wrapping round the front wheels and burning out the engine. Now I have white, straight, fluffy bushels of hair that can't be tamed or fashioned into a style.

Before cancer I would buy furniture that I liked, but now I told Sean to pick the bedroom cabinets as he will be around longer than me to deal with them, so it's best he likes them. He wanted black side cabinets and I wanted grey; we picked the black ones. I won't be here long enough to moan about them.

Before cancer Ashley and I made plans to go to Disneyland and tour America; now we can't make any decisions further away than three months.

After cancer, I don't have to pluck my chin hairs or shave my legs – I have no body hair.

After cancer, I have to make a mental note to check the chances of being alive for a wedding invite that just came through the post. These are things you can't tell people who just want an RSVP for their big day.

After cancer, I no longer wear my favourite lovely underwear; I have to wear pants that fit round my lumpy hernia and make me feel sexless and old, but I have to be glad I'm still alive or people get annoyed at me for complaining that my lingerie doesn't look good. I am sick of people telling me I am lucky to be alive – before cancer nobody told me to be thankful for walking up a flight of stairs. So, fuck cancer.

April 2023 was the big closing gala for the Glasgow International Comedy Festival, which was one of the highlights of my yearly calendar. I would put on a solo show every year and sometimes it would run for three nights, as we sold out Òran Mór Theatre every year. This year I couldn't put on a show, but I was invited to attend the gala show, which also featured the first ever Billy Connolly Spirit of Glasgow Award ceremony. I was nominated alongside amazing worthy comics, like Scott Agnew, Craig Hill, Paul Black and Kieran Hodgson. On the night, the atmosphere backstage was just brilliant. My pal Monica was there and it was good to have her; she was right beside me at my first open spots in London and now she was here at this point in my career. Billy Connolly is literally the God of Comedy in Glasgow, so it was a huge honour just to be nominated.

I went out and did my ten-minute slot, the audience cheered and clapped, and it was amazing to be back amongst my buddies in the dark side stage, laughing and enjoying the atmosphere.

Elaine C. Smith stepped out onto the stage to introduce the winner of the inaugural award. Monica and I watched from backstage as Billy appeared in his on-screen video from his home in Los Angeles.

'The winner of the award – the Billy Connolly Award, believe it or not – is Janey Godley,' he announced with a smile. When he said my name, I froze. 'A worthy winner. A worthy comedian. She's been a pal of mine for about five or six years,' Billy continued, but I was in a daze. I couldn't believe it. I was genuinely amazed; I hadn't thought I could possibly win it. I was reminded daily on Twitter that I was cancelled, and I wasn't funny, and even after selling out a whole tour my confidence was still raw. I could never escape the hatred online, so how could I have won this?

I wept as I walked onstage to a standing ovation. I remember thinking of the first time I met Billy in New Zealand. It had meant everything to me just to sit and have tea with him. Now, here I was about to accept an award in his name. It really felt like a full-circle moment.

I can't recall anything I said or who I thanked or what came out of my mouth. I know I hugged Elaine and couldn't let go. Monica almost ran onstage and grabbed me into a ferocious hug and I had to keep reminding people that I had a sore hernia; big Scott Agnew wept like a baby as he held my face and gave me a gentle squeeze. 'You deserve this, Janey,' he whispered. I was gobsmacked.

After the presentation, I was whisked backstage to a room to meet the press, who had a deadline to meet to report on the award, and on the way I was stopped by a well-known name in the comedy business. They were smiling and, as always, dressed to the nines.

'Congratulations!' they said. I smiled as I clutched the award in my hand. My mind went back to one of my first gigs in the nineties. I had just walked offstage after my set, and that same person told me I was too rude and filthy-mouthed to make it in stand-up. They're well loved in the business, but I never did feel that they ever had my back; even when they hired me for some comedy events there was always that feeling of a side-eye. Too many times I caught just the edge of a sneer when they spotted me at events. I was always never good enough, but then again not everyone can like you, can they?

But things change, eh? Life moves on.

And we all move with it.

Nicola Sturgeon was all over the news in February 2023. She had resigned and now her home had been besieged by the police; they were digging up her front garden, with a CSI tent covering the area, and the press were all camped outside watching the events unfold. I was genuinely waiting on a dead body being excavated but it turned out there were accusations that she had a share in a campervan and had bought some expensive pens. The very things I had been joking about through the pandemic in my voice-overs – the caravan and the clicky pens – were in the news; all we needed was for someone called Frank to hit the press. Well. Boris Johnson had a new baby son and he called him Frank – it was like my comedy sketches were coming to life. My fans even suspected Dolly Parton had given me a shout-out in her latest single, where she sang of Janey having a sign to carry in a fight . . .

We had Nicola booked to interview me for the Glasgow Aye Write festival, which is where authors get interviewed in front of the public to raise money for the libraries.

I was absolutely sure Nicola would not turn up; there was no way her first public appearance after being arrested would be with me. But it seemed that was what was happening, so my agent Chris and I turned up to the Royal Concert Hall with trepidation. What if some of the trolls who had been threatening to protest and shout at the gig turned up? They had been all over social media saying they were coming with the anti-trans mob to give me and Nicola a right telling-off. Then I remembered how cowardly they are, how they can't attend events to shout at women as there are too many supporters who would shout back. They were outnumbered in life as they were online.

The hall sold out, we had one of the biggest audiences at the book festival and I was so excited to see Nicola again.

When we were being introduced the crowd roared; they were on their feet as we came out. I leaned over and whispered, 'Well done' to her. She laughed at me and led me to my seat.

We chatted, laughed, and discussed writing and voice-overs – I even did a voice-over of her there onstage. The audience was amazing, we had a question and answer session and not one person gave us any grief. The hour went by so quickly and I didn't want it to end. Nicola is hugely intelligent, funny and very warm to meet in person. I did suggest we head out in a campervan and tour Scotland; she hasn't said 'no'.

Meanwhile the filming of the documentary continued, with John Archer and his team. Shirley was interviewing me for some segments and they followed us to Belfast, where I was doing a show. Shirley has a really good ear for interviewing and asked me lots of the hard questions as well as the fun stuff. We had a lot to cover, ranging back over the childhood abuse I had suffered, my mum's murder, getting caught with guns in Sean's dad's house, through to leaving The Calton and dealing with the cancellation in 2021. She spared no feelings and went deep and I appreciated that – I wanted this documentary to spare nothing and be truthful.

It was the same with Ashley – when she was being asked about her childhood, she didn't give me or her dad an easy ride. She was very honest about the upside and downside of our parenting. Her candour was refreshing. You always hope you'll do right by your kids but ultimately, in some way or another, you will always fail.

So, now it's late 2023 and I am preparing for more treatment, as my CA-125 number is rising slowly. That might mean I am coping or it may show that the cancer is back. Only the scans will reveal that, and I get four a year. I live like a quarterly electric bill, every three months they let me know if I can carry on. We've just finished doing three sold-out nights at Prestonfield House hotel and it was utterly heavenly – so luxurious to get to stay in a posh hotel that is decorated with heavy oak furniture, tapestries, stuffed birds and giant four-poster beds and has live peacocks in the garden. It looks like the kind of place where Henry VIII is still alive and stalking the corridors looking for a new wife.

What a different experience from my usual Fringe days. I do miss the old days of standing in the Cowgate trying to get fifty people into a wee damp room with Ashley out flyering the crowds. Great memories.

Ashley and I have had a very close relationship her whole life. We laugh at the same things; we cry at the stupidest videos and she's been my biggest cheerleader in my career. I have watched her walk onstage to a huge audience and command a room quickly with her comedy. She is much more self-critical than me; if one joke doesn't land properly, she will ruminate for ages over that. Whereas I just move on and know the audience will laugh so much they will forget the wee mistakes.

She's a ferociously good writer, a brilliant broadcaster and a stunning actor. Of course, I am going to say that; I am proud of my lassie, but she works hard. Her radio show on BBC Radio Scotland on a Friday night was a dead-end slot and through sheer hard work she and her co-host Silent Paul gained a global cult audience with their mixture of comedy, chat and music – it's been going strong for five years. *Dinosaur* was picked up for a six-part series, and she has more writing and acting work in the pipeline.

Ashley has been by my side every step of the way through my comedy career. She was the first to condemn me for fighting online, for the awful tweets, for giving these stupid trolls my time and energy. But as well as being the first to tell me off she is also the first to back me up. We have travelled the world with comedy together; I watched her onstage in Los Angeles rock the room in front of some of the most famous dudes in America and she held her own. The worst moment of my life was telling her I had cancer.

There are no ways to explain properly what it's like to be told you have a terminal disease. You just keep hoping that they'll find a cure but somehow know they won't and that, sooner rather than later, you'll be in a hospice taking morphine and waiting to die without pain. Die without seeing all the things you wanted to experience. Though I'm not sure what they are.

I am lucky that I have seen so much in my life. I did buy that good wine, I did eat in that fancy restaurant. I talked politics, food, Glasgow and swearing on TV with Anthony Bourdain over dinner in Rogano – he made fun of me for being allergic to shellfish; I joked that at least I've never shot up skank in the backstreets of New York.

I did go to Disneyland, I did get to play that venue. I did get to present a BAFTA award, I did get to win many awards, fly first class, have books published, act and write for the National Theatre, see the mountains over Hong Kong, hold my baby daughter after a 27-hour labour, swim in the wonderful oceans off New Zealand, and I got to have tea with Billy Connolly. I am lucky, in many ways.

The best luck I had was going to the Headland Hotel in the eighties, where I came off the birth control pill and conceived our daughter. The rest . . . well, it's been good.

ACKNOWLEDGEMENTS

I want to thank everyone who has been by my side these past three tough years, and the many years before that. Your love and solidarity mean everything to me.